"Being single in today's complex world isn't easy. With straightforward and practical wisdom, *The 10 Best Decisions a Single Can Make* offers biblical help, hope, and clarity. The Farrels have provided a much-needed resource for the single who desires peace and purpose in everyday life."

—LAURA PETHERBRIDGE, speaker and author of *When
"I Do" Becomes "I Don't"* and *The Smart Stepmom*

"As a twentysomething who struggles with maintaining relationships, career, and my place in this world, it's people like the Farrels and books like *The 10 Best Decisions a Single Can Make* that help me get to where I'm called to go."

—RENEE JOHNSON, speaker and author of *Faithbook of Jesus*

"Your next best decision is to buy this book! Encouraging, challenging, and packed with wisdom, this purchase is an easy decision."

—RON L. DEAL, author of *The Smart Stepfamily*

"An immensely practical and powerful book! In their wonderful style, Pam and Bill Farrel share their insights and wisdom to help singles make smarter choices and experience fewer regrets."

—GEORGIA SHAFFER, licensed psychologist
and author of *Taking Out Your Emotional
Trash* and *How NOT to Date a Loser*

"Bill and Pam Farrel truly have a heart for singles, challenging, encouraging, and inspiring them to follow after God wholeheartedly and find fulfillment in His plan and purpose for them."

—CHRISTIN DITCHFIELD, author of *A Way With Words:
What Women Should Know About the Power They Possess*

"*The 10 Best Decisions a Single Can Make* is packed with practical wisdom. The Farrels bless their readers with a biblical roadmap that empowers them to make wise and godly decisions, not only for choosing a life-partner but throughout their life journey, whether they stay single or get married."

—LESLIE VERNICK, licensed counselor and author
of *The Emotionally Destructive Relationship*
and *Lord, I Just Want to Be Happy*

The **10** Best Decisions a Single Can Make

Bill & Pam Farrel

HARVEST HOUSE PUBLISHERS

EUGENE, OREGON

Cover design by Left Coast Design, Portland, OR

Cover photo © D. Hurst / Alamy

THE 10 BEST DECISIONS A SINGLE CAN MAKE
Copyright © 2011 by Bill and Pam Farrel
Published by Harvest House Publishers
Eugene, Oregon 97402
www.harvesthousepublishers.com

Library of Congress Cataloging-in-Publication Data
    Farrel, Bill, 1959-
    The 10 best decisions a single can make / Bill and Pam Farrel.
        p. cm.
    ISBN 978-0-7369-2839-7 (pbk.)
    1. Single people—Religious life. 2. Single people—Conduct of life. 3. Fruit of the Spirit. I. Farrel, Pam, 1959- II. Title. III. Title: Ten best decisions a single can make.
    BV4596.S5F364 2011
    248.8'4—dc22
                                                                        2010032226

Printed in the United States of America

11 12 13 14 15 16 17 18 19 / VP-SK / 10 9 8 7 6 5 4 3 2 1

Contents

One
One single person
One selfless, sacrificing, solo life
One powerful, profound, precious gift
Brought to millions, thousands, hundreds
Brought to you
Life eternal
Jesus
The
One

The One to follow…

To all who are looking for hope, help, and happiness,
may you find these things and so much
more on the pages of this book.

We are profoundly grateful for all we have learned
from our single friends, and we hope this book gives
back some of the insight we have gained from those
who are flying solo, whole, and purposeful.

To Zach and Caleb, our sons, and to
all our nieces and nephews,
"God and one are a majority."
May God do through you what is beyond you.

"Therefore God exalted him to the highest place
and gave him the name that is above every name,
that at the name of Jesus every knee should bow,
in heaven and on earth and under the earth,
and every tongue confess that Jesus Christ is Lord,
to the glory of God the Father."
(Philippians 2:9-11)

One. The first whole number. Complete, not a fraction, not a piece but a whole.

That's how we feel about all those singles who have contributed to this book.

You are transparent. To pen the words on the pages of this book, we have walked alongside you, sometimes literally, as we hiked mountain trails or walked along beaches and lake fronts pondering and praying over the needs, desires, and longings of a single person's heart. Thank you for allowing us to trek beside you and hear all that you were brave and honest to share. Your level of trust in us gave us the ability to wrap God's Word around the single souls worldwide so that they might know they are not alone, that God sees, God knows, and God cares.

You are courageous. We surveyed hundreds of you who have been in our audiences, read our books, and who are our personal friends. You asked us to tackle the hard questions of loneliness, sexuality, financial stress, as well as your place in the church and the world. We have done our best to step up to that call. Thank you for sharing your struggles, and sometimes your tears, so that others might gain from some of your personal losses, hurts, and pains.

You are inspiring. Your faith, your ability to trust God, your belief that He promises you a "future and a hope," moved us and compelled us to tell others of your spiritual journeys so they too could find that same strength for life. Thanks for sharing not just your victories but also the steps, and sometimes the missteps, that created in you an overcoming, triumphant, warrior attitude for good. We were thrilled to see the seeds of greatness in you. Your healthy approach to being single holds together churches, organizations, businesses, and lives with your love and dedication, and for this we are grateful.

You are fun. We celebrated with you, dined with you, played sports and table games with you so you could give us a better glimpse of your lives. In focus groups we laughed and we learned. At dinner parties we enjoyed seeing and hearing your stories of a full, rich, wonderful life. Even as you shared the hard times of feeling lonely, marginalized, or frustrated, you did so with a sense of hope and anticipation about God's unfolding plan for you. We look forward to more parties, celebrations, conferences, and laughs with you all in the days ahead. You are great at creating community—thanks for letting us be a part of that community!

You are profound. One of the singles we respect dearly dared to ask what many want to know but are afraid to ask: "Is there an aspect of knowing God I cannot enter? God uses marriage as an illustration of Christ and the church's relationship to Him. But I have never been a bride. Is there something in the physical closeness that translates into spiritual onesness I cannot enter into?"

Our experience, after spending hours and hours, years and years, ministering to and alongside our single friends who love God is this: There is an intimacy, a closeness, a rich interpersonal dialogue with the Creator that those who are single have the opportunity to create. You are designed with the potential to lean entirely and completely on the God who loves you and created you. A resounding theme we heard you voice was, "Sometimes I feel as if it's me and God against all odds." You are right, and because of this you can experience a special emotional and spiritual intimacy with God. The tendency of married people is to look to another person to ease our stress, lighten our load, and carry our burdens. We have witnessed that valiant singles naturally seek out the deep, precious, unique reliance on God and relationship to Him that all of us should desire. Thanks for desiring more of life and more of God.

You are amazing. We are especially grateful to the singles who work for our publisher, Harvest House, who came to us with the idea of *The 10 Best Decisions a Single Can Make.* Thanks for trusting us to write about your journey and for being a part of the team that created it. And many thanks for being the kind of healthy, whole, positive, merciful, giving, and visionary people others can look up to and emulate. May God continue to do through you what is beyond you so that others might discover lives of courageous faith.

One of our best decisions is knowing and loving you.

CHAPTER 1

Decide to Be Decisive

We make our choices and our choices make us.

Your life is filled with questions only you can answer. These questions include:

- Will you be content with or conflicted about being single?
- What will you do for a career?
- What kind of influence will you have on others?
- How will you develop this influence?
- What will you do to develop healthy friendships?
- Will you take initiative or will you be a follower?
- How will you continue to grow in your personal development?
- How will you handle your dating life?

There are no right or wrong answers to most of these questions, so the answer is determined by a decision on your part. And the quality of your decisions will determine the quality of your life. This is why decision-making is such a vital skill. Amazingly, however, the process for making decisions is a mystery to most people. Ask the average person, "How can you ensure that you're making good decisions?" and you'll probably get vague and insecure answers.

"I don't know."

"I do what feels best and hope it works out."

"Is that even possible?"

"I do what my parents did."

"I don't think about it very much."

One of our friends, radio talk-show host Phil Waldrep, was raised in the Deep South, and he once described a person to us by saying, "That boy was as confused as a termite in a yo-yo!" Now that's confused!

We think most people feel pretty confused in today's world. This is why there is so much emotional turmoil among singles. Our emotions are directly affected by our decisions. If you make sound decisions, you'll feel better about yourself and your life. You may experience peace, elation, contentment, or the like as your heart responds positively to the choice you've made. If you make poor decisions, you may experience turmoil, stress, disappointment, anger, or any one of a hundred negative emotions.

Very few people set out to be indecisive or to make bad decisions, but these two outcomes are epidemic. Counseling offices are filled with people trying to deal with the hurt and disappointments of life. The entertainment world is flooded with stories of shame, selfishness, and self-destructive pursuits. Friendship circles are characterized by people who are frustrated with their underachievement. In our hearts, we all want to make decisions we can believe in and live out wholeheartedly, but few of us know how to develop the skill that makes this possible.

We came across a fascinating website that contains a collection of quotes by a young lady named Michelle. Her list of "Regret and Mistake Quotes" is a fascinating example of how our thoughts compete with each other for attention. Her list contains a number of quotes that inspire healthy decision-making:

- I am who I am today because of the choices I made yesterday.

- When you come to the edge of the light that you know, and you are about to step off into the darkness of the unknown, faith is knowing that one of two things will happen: there will be something to land on, or you will learn how to fly.

- More people would learn from their mistakes if they weren't too busy denying them.

- Anyone who has never made a mistake has never tried anything new.

- Don't be afraid to go after what you want to do and what you want to be. But don't be afraid to be willing to pay the price.

- Just because someone messes up once doesn't mean that within time they can't find a way to change for the better.

- The times in life that seem to be the worst, always turn out for the best!

- Don't put a period where God put a comma.

Alongside of these insightful quotes are a number of others that encourage reckless decisions based on shallow thinking:

- Some mistakes are too much fun to make only once.

- Sometimes we know we shouldn't and that's exactly why we do.

- You're born, you die, and in between you make a lot of mistakes.

- You are my favorite mistake.

- If I don't die the first time, most likely I will do it again.

- I'm a firm believer that sometimes it's right to do the wrong thing.

- I'm not going to apologize for it 'cause the truth is I'd do it again.

- Concern yourself not with what is right and what is wrong, but with what is important.

- If I could go back in time and fix all the mistakes I made, I wouldn't because it has made me who I am today.

- How come dumb stuff seems so smart while you're doing it?[1]

To be sure, decision-making is a journey that is smooth and clear at some times while it is foggy and confusing at other times. Every decision confronts our thinking and tests our ability to do what is best. Every decision is a competition between self-indulgence and self-discipline. We would be the first to say that decision-making is a learning process that can always be improved but never perfected. The journey is well worth it, however. As your skills grow, the path gets clearer and your confidence gets stronger.

The Benefits of Good Decisions

Numerous benefits await those who decide to be decisive. In *The 10 Best Decisions a Man Can Make*, I (Bill) list a number of these benefits:

- We have more energy for the pursuits we care about.
- Decisions make us more efficient.
- Decisions simplify our lives.
- Healthy decisions raise our confidence level.

In addition, consider a few other benefits that come to your life when you learn to be decisive.

You will have better relationships. People you interact with fall into two major categories. Some people enhance your life and some take from your life. People who take from others are obviously less healthy than those who improve the lives of those around them. Choose wisely because unhealthy people don't like healthy environments. They can tolerate them for a while, but eventually they get stressed around healthy people and drift away.

You can develop a healthy environment around you by making sound decisions. The result will be less drama, less turmoil, fewer issues, and more productive conversations. Healthy people will find this stimulating and will want to spend more time with you. Unhealthy people will find it hard to spend time with you and will look for other friends. When you're good at making choices, you don't have to tell people to go away because they don't hang around long enough to be told.

You will have more fun. As you grow in your ability to make decisions, you will get to know yourself better. You'll discover what you like and what you don't like. You'll identify the activities that bring you the most satisfaction. When you have the opportunity to do something fun, you'll quickly know what will work the best.

You will be perceived as a leader. The Bible clearly states that people are like sheep who instinctively follow a shepherd. Jesus said, "My sheep listen to my voice; I know them, and they follow me" (John 10:27). And Mark in his Gospel gives this description of the large crowd who flocked around Jesus: "When Jesus landed and saw a large crowd, he had compassion on them, because they were like sheep without a shepherd. So he began teaching them many things" (Mark 6:34).

Jesus is the chief shepherd, but He utilizes under shepherds to help guide His people. In restoring Peter after his denial of his Savior, Jesus said to him,

> "Simon son of John, do you truly love me?"
> He answered, "Yes, Lord, you know that I love you."
> Jesus said, "Take care of my sheep" (John 21:16).

Peter in turn encouraged the elders to "be shepherds of God's flock" (1 Peter 5:1-3). The point is that sheep look for shepherds to follow, and what separates shepherds from sheep are decisions. Shepherds decide where the best food is, what trails their flock will follow, and the safest places to spend the night. As you become more decisive, people will naturally want to follow your lead.

You will recover quicker from hurts. Unfortunately, we have all been hurt, and we will probably all be hurt again sometime in the future. Some of these hurts are deep-seated wounds experienced during childhood that follow us into adulthood while others are based on mistakes we have made as adults. They haunt us and will halt our progress if left unattended. If they turn to bitterness, they can grow like roots that damage our entire lives. "See to it that no one misses the grace of God and that no bitter root grows up to cause trouble and defile many" (Hebrews 12:15).

Since these hurts are primarily emotional in nature, it helps to make decisions about them. No one logically concludes that living wounded is a good idea. These experiences have such power because they impact the emotional core of who we are and generate intense responses in us. Thinking about the issues doesn't change them, but making decisions about them will.

Avoid the Pitfalls

People fall into several traps that slow personal growth and keep them from healthy decisions:

- They let others make decisions for them that they should be making for themselves.
- They blame poor decisions on others.
- They decide they don't need to make changes because "that's the way they've always been."
- They make excuses for not making decisions.
- They refuse to set priorities that could guide their decisions.
- They are too lazy to make the effort it takes.
- They give in to peer pressure rather than deciding what is best.
- They are not honest about the changes they know deep down need to be made.

Which of these traps are you most susceptible to?

The journey of our lives is filled with decisions. This is the privilege of grace in our lives. The Old Testament contains long lists of what we were required to do but could not do in our own power. In the New Testament, we are given grace, which supplies the power of the Holy Spirit who enables us to choose what was previously impossible. The champion of this message is the apostle Paul. He has a habit of dividing his writings into two sections. The first section is a theological discussion of God's grace. The second section is a discussion of the choices we have based on grace. Here are a couple of examples.

In the book of Romans, Paul spends chapters 1–11 establishing the truth of the gospel and the superiority of grace over the law. In chapter 12, he challenges his readers to make choices motivated by grace. In this one chapter, we are presented with 24 decisions we can make that will enhance our lives, expand our influence, and energize all our relationships. Many of these choices are fun and fulfilling, such as "be transformed by the renewing of your mind" or "rejoice with those who rejoice." We can easily see ourselves making these decisions. Others are remarkable feats of God's grace in our lives, such as "bless those who persecute you" and "be patient in affliction."

Another great example is the book of Galatians. Paul spends the first four chapters establishing the power of grace to save us from our sins. The church was being challenged by teachers to keep their Jewish traditions while adding the gospel to them. Paul argues that grace has fulfilled the law and began a new work in us so that he confidently proclaims, "I have been crucified with Christ and I no longer live, but Christ lives in me. The life I live in the body, I live by faith in the Son of God, who loved me and gave himself for me" (Galatians 2:20). In chapters 5 and 6, he presents another 17 choices believers now have by the power of Christ in them. The most important of these choices is "live by the Spirit, and you will not gratify the desires of the sinful nature" (5:16).

This was impossible before Jesus died, rose again, and sent the Holy Spirit to live in us. Now, however, not only is it possible, it is the most reasonable way of life for someone who knows Jesus. The point Paul is making is that we can choose. We are free from condemnation and have been adopted into the family of God. We now have the privilege to live productive, purposeful, and spiritually powerful lives.

Becoming a Good Decision-Maker

So how do you become a good decision-maker? First and foremost, recognize that decision-making is a skill. It is not a spiritual gift. It is not a unique talent given to a select few. It is not the result of special insight or intellectual prowess. It is a skill in the same way driving, applying makeup, using a computer, or cooking is a skill. Since it is a skill, there are a few guiding thoughts to keep in mind as you seek to improve your ability to make solid choices:

- You will be awkward at first. Every new skill is uncomfortable and feels strange at first. We call it new because you don't have it mastered.

- You get better every time you practice. New skills don't stay new. With each exercise of your will, the skill feels more comfortable. What seemed hard will progress to relatively easy as you spend time working on it.

- You will reach a breakthrough point if you stay at it. Every skill reaches a threshold where it moves from awkward to efficient if you practice it enough times. The difference between those who make good decisions and those who make poor ones has very little to do with talent. Legendary sales trainer Zig Ziglar has said, "The most practical, beautiful, workable philosophy in the world won't work—if you won't."[2] This is never more true than when it comes to choices. If you keep practicing, it will become second nature to you.

- You will get better every time, but you will never be perfect at it. The secret to life is growth rather than perfection. Athletes don't quit because they make mistakes. Business leaders don't sell the business because they make mistakes. Pastors don't give up their churches because they still have things to figure out. In the same way, don't give up because you make a couple of bad choices or you get confused over a decision. Just keep pushing forward to the next decision.

- You will grow faster if you have a team around you. Take this book and ask someone further ahead on the path to meet with you and mentor you. Or challenge a group of friends or your Bible study to go through this book together. Good decision-making is easier if you have people around you who are also making good, wise, healthy choices.

- You will grow faster if you teach someone else how to make decisions. We all struggle with ingrown eyeballs. We evaluate ourselves by ourselves and wonder why we are never satisfied with ourselves. Since none of us are perfect, we stall our growth when we stay focused inwardly. This is one of the reasons the Bible puts such an emphasis on serving one another. When you seek to help others, you evaluate yourself with clearer focus. You'll see that some of your struggles are common with everyone, which will take some of the pressure off you. You'll see that you have progressed in some areas faster than your peers, which will encourage you and help you not be so hard on yourself. You'll also see that explaining a concept to another person helps make it clearer to you. Our thinking can get clogged when we fail to verbalize what we're learning. Passing on what we learn often frees up our thinking again.

There has never been a time in history when the development of this skill has been more important. You live in a relentless flood of information. Every minute of every day you are bombarded by the media, the Internet, business ideas, and casual conversations. New truths are uncovered every day that transform the way we live.

I (Bill) recently watched a movie where the star of the show pulled out a pager. Wow! When I started my career a pager was the hottest communication tool on the market. If you had a pager, you were leading the pack. Today, a pager is laughable, and the same thing will happen with iPhones, Blackberrys, and laptop computers. They will get replaced with something so advanced and so powerful that current technology will become obsolete.

One of the results of the insatiable advancement of knowledge is a never-ending stream of data that requires almost constant decision-making. Strategic decision-making makes life more efficient, which helps you keep up with the torrid pace of progress and gives momentum to your pursuit of God's will. Insufficient decision-making complicates your life and robs your energy.

It makes sense to develop a plan for improving your decision-making skills. The most common method for making decisions, however, is to rely on instinct. You are faced with a decision. Your instincts kick into gear based upon your life experience and emotional programming. A decision occurs to you that feels right. In the absence of any other decisions that seem better, you commit to this course of action.

We act as if decision-making is a magical gift that automatically kicks into gear when we need it. We long for moments of great inspiration when life counts the most only to be disappointed when life doesn't turn out the way we hoped.

There is a better way! We've been equipped with the ability to discern a wise course of action in each decision of our lives. We have been given the mind of Christ (1 Corinthians 2:16), and we can utilize that ability to make effective decisions.

It used to seem to me (Bill) that some people were born with the ability to recognize and pursue healthy decisions while others were doomed to miss strategic decisions or make short-sighted choices. If that were the case, I was sure I was left out of the group born to be strategic. I have since discovered that any time we are faced with a decision, we can perform a number of tests that give guidance, clarity, and confidence to the process.

These tests are the basics of decision-making. The skill is more than the basics, but you can't develop the skill until you have acquired the basics. I remember being exposed to this concept in basketball. Before I could learn offensive schemes, I had to learn how to dribble, pass, and shoot. Once I learned the basics, I could improvise and combine them to perform creative moves. Later in life, I realized this applies to my computer as well. Before I could launch high-powered applications, I had to learn to turn the computer on, type, enter a password, move a mouse, and explore help menus. As I practiced these basics, I was able to get creative with word processing, spreadsheets, video editors, and the like.

Making choices works the same way. Once you get the basics down, you can get creative and progress to the point that sophisticated decisions seem easy.

Decision-Making Skill 1: The Obvious Test

When you're faced with a decision, it's helpful to determine if this is a simple decision or a more complicated choice. So before you put a lot of effort into any decision, ask yourself, "Is this decision so obvious that I'm wasting time thinking about it?" This simple question conserves energy when you encounter obvious decisions. The reason these decisions are obvious is that God has already clearly spoken to these areas of life or they are generally accepted as the best practices. If you put too much into these decisions, you get needlessly sidetracked and train yourself to stall when you ought to push forward. Consider these obvious decisions based on the best practices:

- Brush your teeth every day.

- Dress appropriately for work.

- Pull over when a police car comes up behind you with its lights on.

- Get a good night's sleep regularly.

- If a friend of yours is in the hospital, visit him.

- If a friend or family member gives you a gift, say, "Thank you."

We mentioned that Romans 12 and Galatians 5–6 contain many choices based on the gift of God's grace. Here's a sample of some of the most obvious decisions contained there:

- Renew your mind with God's Word in some way every day (Romans 12:2).

- Hate what is evil (Romans 12:9).

- Be devoted to one another in brotherly love (Romans 12:10).

- Do not be proud, but be willing to associate with people of low position (Romans 12:16).

- Do not use your freedom to indulge the sinful nature; rather, serve one another in love (Galatians 5:13).

- Anyone who receives instruction in the word must share all good things with his instructor (Galatians 6:6).

- As we have opportunity, let us do good to all people (Galatians 6:10).

When you train yourself to do the obvious when it is obvious, you develop habits in your life that become automatic. These habits make your life more efficient as they conserve your energy for more complex choices. They raise your confidence level also as success in simple tasks builds a track record of encouragement for the decisions that are not as obvious.

This sounds so simple, but it has been a huge struggle for people, especially when it comes to relationships. The Bible clearly states, "Do not be yoked together with unbelievers. For what do righteousness and wickedness have in common? Or what fellowship can light have with darkness?" (2 Corinthians 6:14).

While this verse applies to more than romantic relationships, it certainly teaches that believers should not be romantically involved with those who are not like-minded followers of Christ. Sounds simple, but we all know people who have grown emotionally attached to someone who is not good for them. We all have sophisticated ways of deceiving ourselves as we entertain the thought that we will be the exception.

If you're committed to doing what is obvious because it is obvious, you'll avoid this pitfall. If, however, you are trained to follow your emotions more than you follow the obvious, you can easily be allured into a relationship that challenges your spiritual convictions.

Decision-Making Skill 2: The Wisdom Test

In the space below, write down your thoughts to this question: "What is the difference between being smart and being wise?"

Not all decisions are obvious. In fact, most of the decisions we must make require some level of discovery, deliberation, and discernment. This is why the Bible puts such a high value on wisdom, which is the ability to apply what is true to the situations of our lives in a skillful and beneficial way. Most people are intelligent and have the ability to absorb immense amounts of information. In this information age we live in, most people are not even aware of the vast amounts of information they casually discuss every day.

Knowledge, however, is much different than wisdom.

The path for developing wisdom is surrounded with questions. Wise people ask questions with a sincere desire to find answers they can apply to real life. They know they will not get all their questions answered and they are aware that their questions will change as they gain new insight and adjust to the truth they have applied to life. Just like decision-making, wisdom is a skill that can be pursued and developed. The book of Proverbs centers on the notion of wisdom. Notice how many times wisdom is referred to as something to be pursued:

> You who are simple, gain prudence;
>> you who are foolish, gain understanding.
> (Proverbs 8:5)

> Wisdom calls aloud in the street,
>> she raises her voice in the public squares.
> (1:20)

> My son, if you accept my words
>> and store up my commands within you,
> turning your ear to wisdom
>> and applying your heart to understanding,
> and if you call out for insight
>> and cry aloud for understanding,
> and if you look for it as for silver
>> and search for it as for hidden treasure,
> then you will understand the fear of the LORD
>> and find the knowledge of God.
> (2:1-5)

> Blessed is the man who finds wisdom,
>> the man who gains understanding.
> (3:13)

> Get wisdom, get understanding.
> (4:5)

> Wisdom is supreme; therefore get wisdom.
>> Though it cost all you have, get understanding.
> (4:7)

> How much better to get wisdom than gold.
> (16:16)

The obvious question then is, "How do you get wisdom?" James 1:5 gives us some significant insight: "If any of you lacks wisdom, he should ask God, who gives generously to all without finding fault, and it will be given to him." The day you stop asking for wisdom is the day you stop growing in wisdom.

Solomon is a great example for all of us who desire to possess the wisdom to make strategic decisions. He was elevated to a position of overwhelming authority when he was just a young man. "At Gibeon the LORD appeared to Solomon during the night in a dream, and God said, 'Ask for whatever you want me to give you'" (1 Kings 3:5). In humility, he said, "I am only a little child and do not know how to carry out my duties...so give your servant a discerning heart to govern your people and to distinguish between right and wrong" (vv. 7-9). God was pleased to respond, "I will do what you have asked. I will give you a wise and discerning heart" (v. 12).

Daniel is another example of the possibilities when you are willing to ask for wisdom. King Nebuchadnezzar was determined to execute his wise men, including Daniel and his friends, because none of them could interpret a disturbing dream. He and his colleagues asked and God granted, which led to a spontaneous outbreak of gratitude, "I thank and praise you, O God of my fathers: You have given me wisdom and power, you have made known to me what we asked of you, you have made known to us the dream of the king" (Daniel 2:12).

The Wisdom Test, therefore, is a set of questions you ask that helps you apply wisdom when faced with a decision. If you answer yes to all these questions, it's pretty clear that your decision is based on wisdom and you probably ought to proceed forward. If you answer no to all or most of them, you have more rigorous work to do to figure out the best course of action. The goal is to put in the least amount of effort to arrive at an effective decision. The wisdom test will help you conserve energy on decisions that you already possess the wisdom to make.

If the obvious test doesn't make your decision clear, ask the following questions:

- Does this decision line up with my convictions?

- Will the people I respect most agree with this decision? Have I asked them?

- Is this decision based on healthy boundaries that will produce self-respect?
- Will this decision cause personal growth in my life?
- Would I encourage my best friends to make this same decision?

Decision-Making Skill 3: The Priority Test

Some decisions in life require more effort to figure out. You've gone through "The Obvious Test" and "The Wisdom Test," but you still need more evidence that you are making the best decision. This happens when:

- The Bible doesn't specifically address the decision that's before you.
- You have many options to choose from.
- Your two best options are both attractive to you.
- The decision will affect your life for a long time.
- People you respect have differing opinions on how you should decide.

When this occurs, there are simple and practical steps you can take:

Step 1: Write out your decision in a positive way. Describe the decision before you in terms of what you will do if you say yes to this decision. For instance, "I'm thinking about buying a home and looking for a couple of roommates." This is better than, "I need to get out of my parents' home because they are driving me crazy," because it encourages you to think about momentum in your life. You want to leave no room for negative thinking.

Step 2: Make a pro/con list. Create two columns on a sheet of paper. On one side, write down the reasons why you *ought* to take this course of action. On the other side, write down the reasons why this course of action is *not* a good idea.

Step 3: Prioritize the reasons. In both columns, prioritize the reasons you have listed. As you prioritize your thinking, wise decisions begin to make themselves known.

A method that we've found helpful for setting priorities is the ABC system. To use this system, you assign an A to the vital reasons you identify on your list. The supportive reasons get a B. And you mark with a C the reasons you came up with because you're creative and can come up with ideas that don't really affect the decision. Some people prefer to rank the reasons on their list in order of importance (1, 2, 3 and so on). Choose the method you are most comfortable with. For the rest of our discussion, we will assume you're using an ABC system.

Step 4: Compare the high-priority reasons from both lists. Evaluate the A reasons for saying yes with the A reasons for choosing no. If it's a tie, then move to the B reasons to see if the decision becomes clearer. Don't be fooled by quantity. It's quite possible that one list will have more reasons than the other, but quantity is no substitute for quality, and decisions such as this require high-quality conclusions. The list with the most reasons might be the best choice, but it might not. The way to build clarity is to deliberately prioritize the evidence and discipline yourself to focus on the A reasons.

It's Your Turn

What decision are you currently faced with that needs the priority test? Describe the decision in positive terms in the space below. Then on a separate sheet of paper, work through the priority test.

Decision-Making Skill 4: The Brainstorm Test

The vast majority of decisions in your life can be figured out using the Obvious Test, the Wisdom Test, and the Priority Test. Every once in a while, though, you'll encounter decisions or choices that are truly *different* than decisions you've encountered in the past. You're not sure how to get started because you're into new territory with new implications. You have little life experience to draw on and no track record to look back on. In order to tackle these decisions, you need to open yourself up to new possibilities.

This skill is pretty strenuous so you don't want to rely on it very often, but there are times when it is necessary to answer the question, "Have I spent time considering every possible solution I can imagine?" To answer this question requires us to exercise our creativity.

The creativity to identify and explore brand-new possibilities resides in all of us because we are made in the image of a creative God (Genesis 1:1,27). To release this creativity we need to open up our thinking. Most of us have developed either discipline or hesitancy in our thinking. We discipline our thinking so we keep focus on the important responsibilities of life. We hesitate in our thinking because of past mistakes or fear of letting unhealthy desires take over. We need to get beyond these barriers when truly new solutions are necessary. Here are some steps to help unleash this creativity.

Step 1: Brainstorm a solution list. Write down every possible solution you can imagine. Include ideas that seem ridiculous, absurd, or impossible. It is vital at this point that you do not analyze any of these ideas. The brainstorming process is designed to break through the emotional, intellectual, and experiential barriers you have developed. If you analyze or evaluate ideas during the brainstorming process, you will eliminate ideas that could lead to new solutions. The goal here is to get as many ideas on paper as you possibly can in hopes that a new possibility surfaces. If you're having difficulty making a large enough list, ask trusted friends to add their ideas. Do not rush this step! You may even want to take breaks and come back to your list a number of times in order to consider the greatest number of ideas.

Once the brainstorm list is completed, set it aside for a time. This break can last from a few minutes to a few days. The goal of this break is to shift from a brainstorming mentality to an evaluation mentality.

Step 2: Eliminate the ridiculous ideas. Cross out any ideas that are truly ridiculous. Be careful you don't eliminate ideas that *feel* ridiculous to you but are actually good possibilities. Again, you may want to ask friends to help you figure this out. You allowed these ideas to appear on your list to expand your creativity. Now it's time to eliminate them so they don't create clutter as you move forward.

Step 3: Eliminate ideas you are clearly not ready to consider. Some ideas on your list may sound possible, but you know in your heart you would never follow through with them. These ideas may not match your personality or your maturity level. Be careful that you do not eliminate these simply based on your emotional reaction to them. Real change is hard and makes you uncomfortable, so you want to keep challenging ideas on your list. You want to give yourself the freedom, however, to get rid of ideas that you are confident would make you miserable.

For instance, if you are highly creative and love spontaneity, an assembly-line job is not a good idea for you. You may be proficient in the skills required for this job, but it is guaranteed that you will eventually grow bored. Likewise, if you are a task-oriented person who gains great satisfaction from assisting others, being in charge of a company is probably not a good career goal. You may have the insight and drive to succeed for a short period of time in an executive position, but it is unlikely you will enjoy it long term.

The ideas you want to eliminate in this step are those you know in your heart you would never focus on well enough to succeed. You don't want to commit yourself to a course of failure! It's probably wise to have someone you trust help you work through this step so that you don't get rid of ideas you may be afraid of but would likely succeed at if you pursued them. Your trusted friends often have sharper insight into new possibilities for you.

Step 4: Walk the best ideas from your brainstorm list through the Priority Test. Once you've limited your brainstorm list, you'll be left with one or more new courses of action. You now need to evaluate these new ideas. Since you would do this much work only for a life-changing decision, you want to give this process the focus and time it deserves. If you have more than two ideas to consider, work the process until you have only two ideas remaining. Then, instead of a pro/con list, create an idea 1/idea 2 list. List the reasons for each side, prioritize the reasons, and focus your evaluation on the high-priority reasons.

Brad's Move

Brad is a friend of ours who grew up in a loving, God-fearing home with a strange twist. When he was a teenager, his father told his wife and kids that he loved them but that God had led him to begin a new relationship. His father admitted that most people would not understand, but he claimed he had denied it long enough.

It was traumatic to say the least. Questions without answers flooded Brad's mind. The decision-making pallet of his life grew cluttered and confused. How could his father, a man who claimed to be godly, do something so ungodly and bail on his wife and kids? Brad was affected deeply by his father's unhealthy choices. Brad spent many years believing that he was separated from God and unable to ever be worthy of salvation. God is faithful, however, and through a series of events, Brad became convinced that God loved him and had a plan for his life. But he still had lots of questions about how to create a healthy plan and path for his future.

The one thing he knew is that he needed to leave his hometown. There were too many reminders of painful disappointments for him ever to thrive there. Where he should go, however, was a mystery. He didn't realize it at the time, but he informally followed a logical progression for making the decision about where to live.

His first step was the Obvious Test. "I know I need to move. Is it obvious where I should go?"

The answer was, "No. I can live anywhere." God had taught Brad that he could find a home and great friends anywhere through involvement with a group of international Christian singles. All of these young men and women were from other nations, but they had formed relationships with one another that were as good as any loving brothers and sisters.

Then came the Wisdom Test. "Are all the people I trust telling me to move to the same place? Is there a place to move that looks better to me than other places? Is there an opportunity before me that appears to be a God-given appointment?" Again the answers were all no, leaving Brad with the need to be more deliberate about the decision.

As he was considering this decision, he read these words in the Bible, "The Lord had said to Abram, 'Leave your country, your people and your father's household and go to the land I will show you'" (Genesis 12:1). This verse stuck in his mind, so he began praying, "Lord, is that what I'm supposed to do?" He couldn't think of a reason not to at least consider this, so he fasted and prayed about it.

He wrote out, "Should I pack what I own into my car, leave my hometown, and move to the place that God points out to me?" He came up with the following reasons for saying yes to this opportunity:

- My best chance to live an excellent life is away from my hometown.
- I am single.
- I believe God is leading me this way.
- I have a car.
- I have been trained to make friends.
- My faith is strong.

He recognized the following reasons for saying no to this opportunity:

- I will be without a job when I arrive wherever I'm going.
- Other people will think I'm crazy.
- It could be hard to find work.
- I may not know anyone wherever it is that I'm going.

As he thought through the issues, he concluded that the A priorities from the yes side were:

- My best chance to live an excellent life is away from my hometown.
- I believe God is leading me this way.

The only A priority from the no side was "I will be without a job when I arrive wherever I'm going." The fact that he was single minimized this for Brad. He knew he could live simply and work in humble positions until he could find more fulfilling employment. The other idea that bothered him was that others might think he was a little crazy for taking a step that might look reckless. He knew intellectually that people's opinions of him were not nearly as important as God's opinion, but he had never really tested that theory. The idea that God was leading him got Brad excited by the possibility of courageously walking by faith. Teamed together with the conviction that he needed to get away from his hometown, the decision became surprisingly clear.

He was ready to settle anywhere that might hold the promise of a stable living, even if it meant enduring a harsher climate than the one he was used to living in. He initially set his sights on a Midwestern state where job opportunities abounded. He felt prepared to endure the harsh winters as long as he could find a reasonable livelihood there. In the meantime, Brad's aunt heard that he was determined to leave his hometown, so she invited him to move clear across the country to live with her and her husband until he could find work.

Brad accepted his aunt's generous offer. He packed his 1986 Toyota Celica and headed out. "Okay, God, I know where I'm going, but I'm completely dependent on You to provide a job and friends."

Although Brad was prepared to endure the Midwestern weather, God had set his course for the milder climate of South Florida. He joyfully anticipated those five days of driving, deciding to spend the entire time in silence, talking to Jesus as he drove across the country.

Looking back, Brad has concluded this was one of the best decisions he ever made. He still talks fondly of the five days of prayer as one of the high points of his spiritual journey. His aunt and uncle welcomed him with open arms, and he found a job shortly after he arrived. Within two months, he had an apartment of his own and connected with a church. He has led small groups, made great friends, and been consistently employed ever since. More importantly, his faith has grown strong, and he has found a life of freedom and focus.

Getting away from the town that was flooded with painful memories set him free to enjoy God's design for his life. Asking the question, "How do I want to live?" was much easier in this new environment. He knows this is not the only way to overcome family pain, but it was God's way for him.

Just for Fun

Doctor: Well, I have good news and bad news.
Man: Can I have the good news first?
Doctor: You have 24 hours to live.

Man: What! How can there be any worse news?
Doctor: Well, I forgot to call you yesterday.[3]

You have more than 24 hours to live and you are a decision-maker. A great journey awaits, and you can figure it out. Let's go!

CHAPTER 2

Decide to Walk with Jesus

"The fruit of the Spirit is love…"

GALATIANS 5:22

I t has often been said, "It isn't what you know; it's who you know." There's a lot of truth in that statement. The best opportunities in your career come from personal connections with people. You can find jobs through the paper or a job fair, but the positions you find through referrals are better and more satisfying. You find your best friends through introductions from others in your circle of influence. The people in your life determine the quality of your life.

Jim Burns of HomeWord Radio tells this story:

> Shortly after World War II came to a close, Europe began picking up the pieces. Much of the Old Country had been ravaged by war and was in ruins. Perhaps the saddest sight of all was that of little orphaned children starving in the streets of those war-torn cities.
>
> Early one chilly morning an American soldier was making his way back to the barracks in London. As he turned the corner in his jeep, he spotted a little lad with his nose pressed to the window of a pastry shop. Inside the cook was kneading dough for a fresh batch of doughnuts. The hungry boy stared in silence, watching every move. The soldier pulled his jeep to the curb, stopped, got out, and walked quietly over to where

the little fellow was standing. Through the steamed-up window he could see the mouth-watering morsels as they were being pulled from the oven, piping hot. The boy salivated and released a slight groan as he watched the cook place them onto the glass-enclosed counter ever so carefully.

The soldier's heart went out to the nameless orphan as he stood beside him. "Son...would you like some of those?" The boy was startled.

"Oh, yeah...I would!"

The American stepped inside and bought a dozen, put them in a bag, and walked back to where the lad was standing in the foggy cold of the London morning. He smiled, held out the bag, and said simply, "Here you are." As he turned to walk away he felt a tug on his coat. He looked back and heard the child ask quietly: "Mister...are you God?"[1]

The most important person you will ever meet is Jesus. But sometimes we get confused about who Jesus is.

One father was home on furlough from the mission field, and he enrolled his son in preschool. The teacher invited the dad to come to the classroom and share the true meaning of Easter with the preschoolers. The dad thought he would find out what the kids knew already, so he asked, "Who knows the meaning of Easter?"

One little girl raised her hand, "Is it the day we dress up in costumes and people give us candy?"

"No honey, that is not Easter. I think you're thinking of Halloween."

A boy eagerly raised his hand. "Is it the day my mom cooks all day and dad watches football all day?"

"Nope, that sounds like Thanksgiving."

"I know," a little girl chimed in, "Easter is the day we have a big tree and lots of presents for me."

"No sweetie, that's Christmas."

Finally the man's son, tired of the game, said, "Easter is the day that Jesus died on the cross for our sins—you know, the bad things we say and do. Then they took him down off the cross and they laid him in the tomb."

The father was feeling proud that his son knew the real meaning of

Easter, then the boy added, "And when He comes out of the tomb, if He sees His shadow we have six more weeks of winter!"

What's Your Jesus View?

We have noticed that when it comes to knowing Jesus, people fall into one of five categories. They either won't consider Him, they wonder about Him, they wave to Him, they wild card Him, or they walk with Him.

Won't Consider Him

Some people simply won't consider Jesus. The heart of mankind is naturally proud and selfish. Ever since the fall of Adam and Eve, people have thought they know better than God. They make up their own rules and act as if they are the center of their existence. They would rather stubbornly hold on to their conclusions than hand over their destiny to a Savior. Their hearts are hard toward God because they don't want to be under anyone's authority. They are self-reliant and don't want to even consider that the emptiness in their soul is because Jesus is not there. They are either indifferent or offended by conversations about God, salvation, heaven, and truth.

The Bible says, "The god of this age has blinded the minds of unbelievers, so that they cannot see the light of the gospel of the glory of Christ, who is the image of God" (2 Corinthians 4:4). It is one of the sad realities of life that those who refuse to believe develop spiritual blindness. They don't recognize the gospel as true, and they think Jesus is just another man who lived in history.

Many people who refuse to know Jesus appear to do fine in life. They have successful careers, active social lives, and loving families. They volunteer in their communities and contribute to worthy causes. They may have some inconvenient habits, but it's hard to argue with the success they've enjoyed. They have a hard time seeing their need for a Savior because they have done so well on their own.

Others who refuse to know Jesus are miserable. They complain, underachieve, make poor decisions, and experience painful relationships. They lack peace and prosperity. They multiply pain and disappointment. Even in their desperation, they are unwilling to admit their need for a Savior as they relentlessly pursue their futile way of living.

Wonder about Him

The second group of people wonder about Jesus. They notice that others sincerely love Him and have found peace and purpose. They admire these people who seem to have unusual spiritual strength. They have a hard time, however, accepting that this could be true for them.

For some, childhood memories haunt them with self-doubt. Growing up they heard a lot of negative comments from the people who loved them the most. They have often wondered if their parents really loved them. They are pretty sure they did, but then wonder how someone who loved them could have said the things they said.

"You're ugly. You're stupid. You never do anything right."

Kids don't have filters to help them process statements such as these. Kids are prepackaged to believe their parents, so we get emotionally attached to these evaluations. We start our journey believing these must be true or our parents would not have said them. At some point we begin to evaluate these statements. We conclude that our parents told us lies, but we have a hard time dismissing them because we are emotionally attached to them. We feel as though there must be something to them since our parents said them so often, even though we know they came from our parents' own pain or insecurity.

If this is you, there is a way to do battle with these thoughts. First, identify the statements that have made such a profound impact on your self-image. You don't have to remember everything that was said, but you do need to recognize the statements that have stuck with you and shaped who you are. Some of these statements are positive, and you need to affirm them. For each statement that added value to your life, write it down and read it out loud every day for the next 30 days. These will be easy for you to believe since you are emotionally attached to them, so use them to keep momentum going in your growth.

The statements that were negative are much harder to put into perspective. Dealing with them is relatively simple, but it isn't easy. It's simple because God has designed life in a way that works. He doesn't want life to be a hidden mystery that requires exceptional skill to figure out.

The challenge comes from the emotional complexity of our most important relationships. Learning is a combination of thoughts, decisions, and emotions. Our development begins with our thoughts. We are bombarded throughout our lives with information about who we are, which forms the landscape from which we evaluate our lives. As we are exposed to this information, we make decisions about what we believe. With every decision we make, our emotions are moved. If we believe the messages we hear are true, we will develop an emotional attachment to the information. If we believe the messages are false, we will emotionally filter them out of our conclusions about who we are and the value we possess.

As a child, you had no choice but to believe the messages you received from your family. If they were positive, thank God for them and enjoy the momentum they bring to your life. If they were negative, you will need to make some decisions to unwind the emotional power they hold over you. Here are some suggestions for how to make that happen.

Step 1: Make a list of the thoughts that have the biggest impact on you. We suggest you write these down so you don't have to rely on your memory or your emotional reactions to the thoughts to clearly identify them.

Step 2: Identify the statements that are positive. We all have a tendency to mix all the messages together so they form one big message rather than separate thoughts that can be evaluated and modified. Thank God for the positive messages. These are gifts to you since they have strong emotional momentum behind them and are easy to believe.

Step 3: Renounce the negative statements. As you consider the messages you've grown up with, you'll realize that some of them are just not true. They sprouted out of the brokenness in the hearts of your loved ones. Since they are human and are subject to the same troubles in life that everyone has to deal with, it is predictable that they had inconsistencies and deficiencies in their ability to raise you. The best thing you can do is to commit to live better. It is likely they loved you very much and were trying to do the best with what they had to work with. You can honor your family most by minimizing the impact of their weaknesses. To do this, you have to boldly and persistently proclaim that false statements are false statements. It's best if you say these out loud because your learning is strengthened when your ears hear your voice saying what is true.

Step 4: Replace the negative messages with new messages. Our minds never work in a vacuum, so we must embrace new information if we are ever to make real change in the way we look at ourselves. The apostle Paul tells us, "Do not conform any longer to the pattern of this world, but be transformed by the renewing of your mind. Then you will be able to test and approve what God's will is—his good, pleasing and perfect will" (Romans 12:2).

Notice this verse doesn't talk about just adding information. Instead, the goal is transformation through the renewing of your mind. That is real change, not just a cover-up for what you don't like. To accomplish this, we must train our minds to grasp God's will. Specifically, this means that we replace false thoughts with God's thoughts. We grew up with what humans thought of us, but we are not limited to this information. God has a lot to say about who we are in Christ. For instance, the Bible says that we are:

- The salt of the earth (Matthew 5:13)
- The light of the world (Matthew 5:14)
- More valuable than birds (Luke 12:24)
- Already clean (John 15:3)
- Partners with God [branches of the vine that hold the fruit for others to enjoy] (John 15:5)
- Friends of Jesus (John 15:14)
- Servants of the Most High (Acts 16:17)
- Called to belong to Jesus (Romans 1:6)
- Weak in our natural selves (Romans 6:19)
- Free from condemnation (Romans 8:1-4)
- Children of God [you can call Him Daddy] (Romans 8:14-16)
- Heirs of all that belongs to Christ (Romans 8:17)
- More than conquerors (Romans 8:37)
- God's handiwork (Ephesians 2:10)
- God's temple [the place where the Holy Spirit has chosen to live] (1 Corinthians 3:16-17)
- A vital part of the body of Christ (1 Corinthians 12:21-27)

- Christ's ambassadors (2 Corinthians 5:20)
- Sons of God and heirs of all that belongs to Christ (Galatians 3:26; 4:6-10)
- Members of God's household (Ephesians 2:19)
- Children of the light (Ephesians 5:8)
- Living stones (1 Peter 2:5)
- Chosen people who are viewed by God as royalty (1 Peter 2:9-10)

This is what God says about you. He does not ask you to earn it and He does not base it on your performance. This is His conclusion of who you actually are once you come to Christ as your Savior. It is a package deal, and it is stated by the author of truth.

This is very useful because you need an intellectual and emotional way to do battle with the negative thoughts that have been significant in your development. You can review good information for years without seeing any real change in your life. Transformation requires decisions based on good information that energizes your emotions. When this happens, you become emotionally attached to new thoughts.

God's thoughts are a powerful engine for change because you can say, "That is what others have said about me, and this is what God says about me. Who is smarter, God or those other people?" When you quote God as the authority of who you are, you create powerful leverage in your heart. Since He is all-knowing, the information He shares is completely trustworthy. Since He is all-loving, His perspective is one of care. Since He is holy, He can never lie, and since He is all-powerful, He can accomplish everything He promises. We can try to find other people's words to build us up, but there is no more powerful expert on who you are than God Himself, and He has already spoken.

The challenge comes down to volume. The messages holding you back were said to you over and over in the midst of highly charged situations. Each time you heard the negative messages was like turning up the volume on the background music of your life. You are used to this sound, and it's loud enough to drown out messages that could otherwise change your life.

When you repeat a new thought about who you are, it turns up the volume on the new message. The problem is that you have to hear the new message over and over until the volume of the truth gets close to the same volume as the old messages. This is why many people try but conclude this doesn't work for them. They have read what God says, but because the change wasn't fast enough, they concluded it didn't work. Rather than realize the volume wasn't high enough, they conclude that something is wrong with them. What is really needed is repetition. The negative conclusions were learned through repetition, and the change will happen through repetition.

This is what we mean when we say it's simple but not easy. Finding what is true about you is simple because God has already written it down in the Bible. Saying what is true about you is simple because God put it in simple language. Saying it once without any tangible results is difficult. Saying it 10 times with very little tangible results is difficult. Staying at it until your heart shifts to the new messages requires dedication, discipline, and daring faith to believe what is true when you can't feel it.

You don't have to wonder anymore. God does love you. God does have a wonderful plan for your life. God does want to help you make great decisions for your life.

Wave to Jesus

The third group of people are those who wave to Jesus. We live and lead in Southern California, and we call this attitude "surf's up."

Kent (also known as Moondoggie) and three of his surfing buddies have gone surfing every Saturday for nearly 30 years. One Saturday, the guys were surfing near a highway when a funeral procession drove by. Well, Kent stood up on his board and placed his hand over his heart. This procession was huge and took nearly five minutes to pass. Once it passed, Kent sat down on his board and waited for the next wave. Needless to say, his buddies were floored by his actions.

One of them finally said, "That sure was a respectful thing you did there when they went by."

Kent replied, "It seems the least I could do seeing as how I've been married to the woman for over 30 years!"

Skewed priorities!

We live right by the ocean, and the surfer attitude permeates the culture. It's not unusual for us to say to someone, "Hey, love to see you Sunday at church." The typical response is, "Yeah, I've been meaning to get there," or "Sure thing!" Then with a wink and a wave they're off. We know that means, "I'll be there if something better doesn't come along."

I will have a job, work, have friendships, go to church, volunteer—unless the surf's up. Then I'm out in the ocean. Man, there are priorities, and surfin' is one of them.

And it isn't just surfers or those who live in Southern California who have this attitude. It permeates our culture. It's common for people to wave at Jesus from across the street, from the window of their cars, as they go about their daily routines. There is no real interaction, just a wave, a wink, and a nod.

People love God and trust Him as their Savior, but they are casual in their pursuit of spiritual growth. They attend church regularly but do not make it a high priority. They make minimal commitments to activities that focus on growth, such as Bible studies and small group meetings. They read the Bible but don't work very hard at applying it to their lives. Their devotions are short and their personal prayer times are shallow.

This is where many people live. They're not opposed to Christ, and they genuinely believe He is the Savior of the world. They think fondly about Him and don't want to do anything that would be hurtful to Him. They just lack the intensity to pursue an active, vital relationship with Him. They're like acquaintances who pass each other at school, at work, or at the mall. They smile and wave at each other and may even stop to have a short conversation. They would, however, never spend all day together or go on vacation together.

They are content with this arrangement because there is no great desire to have anything but an acquaintance. They get kind of irritated when they think that Jesus is trying to tell them what to do. They're aware He has the authority to do so, but they haven't grown to trust Him enough to hand over control.

Why wave when you can have a relationship that will truly bless, encourage, strengthen, and enrich your life?

Wild Card Jesus

In card games, the wild card is a card you can assign any value you want. People who wild card Jesus tell God what to do and who they want Him to be. It's as if they think they can decide what role God will play in their lives. A lot of people design their own religion or their own version of Christianity. If they don't like a verse, they just ignore it. If a commandment is hemming in their enjoyment of a sin, they just push the mute button on the Holy Spirit. It they feel confined by just one road to heaven, they embrace all roads.

We have seen people with a crucifix, a Star of David, a Muslim crescent, a new age crystal, and Buddha all on one necklace. All they needed to add was a rabbit's foot and a four-leaf clover for good luck. Some people are authentic Christian believers, but they've drifted from an intimate relationship with Christ, and going to church has become a show, a game, a way to make business contacts, a place to meet chicks, a location to highlight their talents, or a venue to boss people around.

Wild carding Christ is a dangerous position to take. The Bible gives some clear warnings to those who change God's Word, teach false doctrine, or twist what it means to worship:

> Woe to those who call evil good
>   and good evil,
> who put darkness for light
>   and light for darkness,
> who put bitter for sweet
>   and sweet for bitter.
> Woe to those who are wise in their own eyes
>   and clever in their own sight.
>   (Isaiah 5:20-21)

"Woe to you, teachers of the law and Pharisees, you hypocrites! You shut the kingdom of heaven in men's faces. You yourselves do not enter, nor will you let those enter who are trying to...

"Woe to you, teachers of the law and Pharisees, you hypocrites! You give a tenth of your spices—mint, dill and cummin. But you have neglected the more important matters of the law—justice, mercy and faithfulness...

"Woe to you, teachers of the law and Pharisees, you hypocrites! You clean the outside of the cup and dish, but inside they are full of greed and self-indulgence" (Matthew 23:13,23,25).

People will be lovers of themselves, lovers of money, boastful, proud, abusive, disobedient to their parents, ungrateful, unholy, without love, unforgiving, slanderous, without self-control, brutal, not lovers of the good, treacherous, rash, conceited, lovers of pleasure rather than lovers of God—having a form of godliness but denying its power. Have nothing to do with them (2 Timothy 3:2-5).

Here are some questions you might want to ask yourself to see if you have any tendencies to wild card Christ:

- Do you look forward to the acclaim you get each week at church more than you look forward to worshipping God?

- Are you creating your own version of power instead of thanking God for His overcoming power?

- Are you looking to rise in leadership in a church or a Christian organization, yet walk by opportunities every day to help others because no one might see or know you're doing those acts of kindness?

- Do you love yourself, your way, your money more than you love God, God's Word, and God's ways?

- Do you read and interpret God's Word in ways that meet your own needs or agenda?

- Are you leading anyone else down your misguided path: friends, someone you date, coworkers? Are you setting an example that would cause others to sin or are you encouraging others to join with you in your sin?

Wild carding God might lead to a wild consequence, one you might not enjoy at all. "Don't be misled: No one makes a fool of God. What a person plants, he will harvest" (Galatians 6:7 MSG). What you sow, you reap. So the big decision is, "What do I want to reap?"

Walk with Jesus

Finally, some people walk with Jesus. Many references in the Bible compare a relationship with Him to walking with Him. This is a common expression because walking was the main mode of transportation during the life of Jesus. The New International Version contains 21 references to Jesus walking. Many of these involve some of the most important events in His earthly ministry.

One of His greatest miracles involved walking: "When they had rowed three or three and a half miles, they saw Jesus approaching the boat, walking on the water; and they were terrified" (John 6:19). One of his most effective teaching moments involved walking: "As they talked and discussed these things with each other, Jesus himself came up and walked along with them" (Luke 24:15). His recruiting of the men who would change the world involved walking: "As he walked along, he saw Levi son of Alphaeus sitting at the tax collector's booth. 'Follow me,' Jesus told him, and Levi got up and followed him" (Mark 2:14).

Jesus' style was patterned after the rabbinic form of education. Rabbis would train their followers as they "walked along the way." They would live together at times. They would share meals together. They would travel as a group. The students would observe the way their mentor lived, interacted with people, and made decisions. The teacher would use everyday experiences to teach the important principles of life. Rather than meet in a formal classroom, they would walk together through life and learn as they went.

Walking with Jesus was, therefore, the greatest privilege He could offer. As people grew to understand that Jesus was a wise and authoritative rabbi, they longed to be invited into His circle of influence. To walk with Jesus meant to learn from Him, observe Him, interact with Him, ask Him lots of questions, and be entrusted with His purpose. As the disciples walked with Jesus, they enjoyed an adventure they could never have orchestrated themselves. They helped with miracles, witnessed impossible healings, heard authoritative teaching, and watched as people were set free. Walking with Jesus exposed them to a bigger life than they ever imagined.

Want to Go for a Walk?

So why would anyone not want to walk with Jesus? We believe it's because walking with Jesus brings us to the light. Jesus said, "I am the light of the world. Whoever follows me will never walk in darkness, but will have the light of life" (John 8:12). As the disciples walked with Jesus, the truth about life became obvious. It was fun when the truth was easy. The day the disciples fed the 5000 with a small boy's lunch was a fun day. The day when Jesus turned water into wine was a fun day. Days like these brought a smile to their faces and created memories that were fun to tell over and over.

Not all the days were like this, however. When Jesus argued with the Pharisees and made them mad enough to plot against Him was not a fun day. When Jesus confronted the rich young ruler and watched him walk away was not a fun day. The day the disciples could not cast out a demon because of their lack of spiritual wisdom and power was not a fun day. The day they saw their master arrested on false charges was definitely not a fun day.

The truth is inconvenient at the same time that it is encouraging because the human race is flawed and corrupt. As a result, people are capable of great accomplishments and great harm. The truth uncovers both, so when you walk in the light, you encourage those who do right and bring conviction to those who do wrong. Some people love to see you coming while others will potentially hate you simply for being a good person.

It is, therefore, a courageous decision to walk with Jesus. You will make this choice if you think it's worth it. There are certainly some great benefits to walking with Jesus. We will develop great friendship with others who are walking the same road, and we will live free from the nagging weight of sin's accusations. "If we walk in the light, as he is in the light, we have fellowship with one another, and the blood of Jesus, his Son, purifies us from all sin" (1 John 1:7).

At the same time, we will experience the same kinds of difficulties that Jesus experienced. "'No servant is greater than his master.' If they persecuted me, they will persecute you also" (John 15:20).

Once you've experienced the adventure, however, there is no going back. You come to realize this is the normal way to live: "Since we live by the Spirit, let us keep in step with the Spirit" (Galatians 5:25). So, despite the risks, many choose to walk with Jesus because they are intensely interested in Jesus and believe He is "the way, the truth and the life" (John 14:6). They are faithful in the pursuit of their spiritual growth as they search the Bible for truth about life. They actively invite Jesus into every activity and consult Him often on their decisions and the inevitable interruptions of life. They share their opinions with Him and ask Him for advice. In a word, they look for ways to get Jesus involved in every aspect of their lives.

The Climb

One of the most important steps in walking with Jesus is the decision to invite Him into the struggles of our lives. Just as a hike up a mountain trail is easier with a buddy, so is walking through tough days easier with Christ. As you read this, you may be struggling with gossip or pornography or insecurity or selfishness or a long list of other self-destructive options. Our natural response is to hide these struggles from our treasured Savior. We don't want to disappoint Him; we want Him to be proud of us. So we attempt to withhold information. We know this is silly, because God is well aware of all that is going on with us. But we tend to withhold anyway. Walking with Jesus takes on remarkable value when we invite Him to be involved in our common struggles.

One of our common struggles revolves around relationships. We all long to be loved and to give love. Some of you reading this book are content to express this in friendships, and the thought of being single for the rest of your life is attractive. Many of you, however, are frustrated as you live with the nagging desire to be in a romantically satisfying relationship. This desire leads to consistent struggles with lust and loneliness. We see members of the opposite sex who are attractive to us, and our imagination runs wild. We imagine involvement with this person that brings either sexual, social, or emotional satisfaction. We are ashamed by these thoughts and impulses, so we keep silent about them in prayer.

Walking with Jesus calls us to the opposite. Since Jesus is the most trusted person who ever lived, He can be trusted with our shortcomings. Instead of trying to hide, we encourage you to be bold with your Savior. Pray something like, "Jesus, I am really struggling with this. Please meet the need in my life that I think this person can meet." This doesn't take the place of looking up helpful verses or disciplining ourselves to avoid temptation, but it is certainly part of the journey.

None of us will reach a place of perfection on earth so it makes sense to make this part of our relationship with Jesus. He already knows, so we aren't telling Him anything new. We are, however, raising the transparency level of our interaction with Him.

What are your most common struggles? Right now, invite Jesus to join you in the midst of these struggles.

It's Your Decision

Why is the question about Jesus so important? We are all talented enough to come up with our own plans and to solve most of our own problems. We live in a day and age with unprecedented technological advances. We can access information and solutions faster than any previous generation. In such an advanced environment, why should we consider walking with Jesus as the primary focus of our lives?

He is the author of life. Our lives were His idea: "all things were created by him and for him" (Colossians 1:16). In His creativity and compassion, He chose to create you. He chose for you to be alive in this generation. He chose to give you the gifts and talents you possess. He chose to place you in the family in which you grew up. He chose to give you a love for certain things while you are naturally disinterested in other areas. These are all aspects of your life you could never have chosen for yourself. We have the awesome privilege of making choices, but we do not get to choose everything. We have a Creator who made many of these decisions on our behalf.

As the author of life, Jesus stands apart from everyone else. We all reflect His image, but no one is fully like Him. He is smarter, more creative, more powerful, and more authoritative than anyone else because He alone put it all in motion. It just makes sense to interact as often as possible with the one who made life if we are given the opportunity. Men and women who have built large organizations, large reputations, or large circles of influence are inaccessible to the average person. This is not true of Jesus. He is the greatest leader and innovator the world has ever known, and yet He has plenty of time and focus to give to anyone who wants to walk with Him.

He is the best advisor in life. All of us need advice along our journey. We are consistently faced with questions, problematic situations, and unexpected obstacles. At times we know exactly how to respond, but often the best course of action is a mystery. We know we must make a decision, but we lack the assurance that our solution is going to be effective. Our need for good advisors is evidenced by the questions we commonly ask:

- What should I do for a career?

- Should I get married? If so, how will I know when I've found the right person?

- What type of ministry should I get involved with?

- How do I know if a potential friend is a healthy person?

- Where should I live?

- What church should I attend?

These are all choices that have options. Success in these pursuits requires wisdom, courage, skillful evaluation, and the ability to prioritize preferences. These are exactly the situations that require trusted advisors who have sufficient life experience, discernment, and empathy.

No one has more of these vital characteristics than Jesus. He knows what it's like to grow up in a family, build a business, develop a ministry, make friends, and stand for your convictions in the midst of conflict and criticism. He knows what it's like to be rejected and betrayed by people who are close to you. He knows what it's like to be falsely accused. He knows what it's like to die. He even knows what it's like to rise from the dead. You have no other friend like this!

He is everyone's accountability partner. We all do better in our lives when we know that we will answer to someone else. As kids, our behavior was better if we knew our parents would discipline us if we did wrong. Among our friends, we live stronger if we're willing to let them confront us when our choices are self-destructive. In most work environments, people get more done when a supervisor regularly gives evaluations and corrective measures.

Whether we realize it or not, we all have an accountability partner in

Jesus. In an ultimate sense, "each of us will give an account of himself to God" (Romans 14:12). At the end of our lives, each of us will stand before Jesus and honestly discuss what we did and why we did it.

Jesus is much more active than this, however. He isn't waiting until our lives are over to get involved. He's involved today. First of all, "He rewards those who earnestly seek him" (Hebrews 11:6). Those who walk with Jesus and diligently seek to stay in sync with Him find that He provides encouraging incentives. He provides clear direction (Psalm 32:8), freedom from worry (Matthew 6:33), confidence (Psalm 9:10; Psalm 34:4), the resources we need (Psalm 34:10; Philippians 4:19), joy (Psalm 69:32; Galatians 5:22), peace (Galatians 5:22; Philippians 4:6-7), and the list goes on. It would take the rest of this book (and it would have to be a very large book) to detail the blessings God brings to the lives of those who seek Him. Jesus actively looks for ways to reward those who walk with Him.

Midcourse Correction

The other side of accountability is correction. Since we're all imperfect, we make mistakes, miss opportunities, and manipulate others. We all have blind spots.

Jim Smith was driving erratically, so the highway patrol pulled him over. They gave him the battery of tests for drunken driving and were about to give him a breath test when an accident happened on the other side of the road.

"Stay here," they said to Jim.

But Jim thought, *This is my chance to escape.* So he got in the car, drove home, and parked the car in the garage.

Then he went inside and told his wife, "If anyone asks, I've been home sick all day." Jim put on his pj's and went to bed.

A few hours later there was a knock on the door. It was the highway patrol.

"Ma'am, someone at this address was pulled over today, and we were writing up the citation when an accident happened. Could we see your husband?"

She went to get her husband, who by now was faking a cold and cough.

"Are you Jim Smith?" the officer asked.

"Why yes, I am."

"Were you pulled over and cited today for a traffic violation?"

"Oh no, sir, I've been sick all day."

"Sir, someone with your name, someone using this address was pulled over today. Perhaps if I just saw the car it could clear things up."

So Jim led the officer out to the garage thinking, *I am totally going to get away with this. It's been hours, and the engine is nice and cold.* Then Jim threw open the garage door, and there in his garage was the highway patrol car with its lights still flashing.

Jim had a blind spot. We all do. The lights are flashing in our garage too.

When our blind spots and imperfections show up, we must make course corrections if we want to continue to walk in the light. For this reason, "the Lord disciplines those he loves" (Hebrews 12:6). The process begins with self-discipline, which is produced by the Holy Spirit in us as we walk with Jesus (Galatians 5:23). When self-discipline breaks down, Jesus confronts us about attitudes, behavior, and choices that undermine our ability to live out our purpose.

Make no mistake, your Savior is dedicated to leading you in the pursuit of the purpose He created you for. When you get off track He will assign significant resources to steer you back. He will use Scripture passages, inner turmoil, or comments from friends to get your attention and stir your heart. He will find ways to point out errors that hold you back with the goal of increasing your effectiveness. If you respond to the initial correction, He will encourage you and empower you to move forward. If you resist, the correction intensifies in an attempt to break down your stubbornness.

I (Bill) was recently reminded as I helped my oldest son move across country that course corrections hold great value. We had two vehicles and three drivers. One of the vehicles was a rental truck that held all my son's worldly belongings. On the third day, we stopped for dinner in Amarillo, Texas. After we got back on the road, the truck would not accelerate beyond 50 miles per hour. Our male instincts told us to push forward, so we debated longer than we should have about whether to call the rental company. By the time we called, we were about 15 miles outside of Amarillo. We were told to pull over to the side of the road and wait for a technician.

None of us were happy about the delay. We grumbled and paced along the grass at the rest area. We all made suggestions about how to fix the problem, but we finally resigned ourselves to the fact that we were just going to have to wait.

As we waited, we watched dark clouds gather on the horizon. At first it was fascinating to watch this thunderstorm form. It was still some distance away, but it was ominously powerful and beautiful. Then it started to close in on us. The wind picked up, lightning bolts shot out of the sky quickly followed by the rumble of thunder. To keep from getting soaked, we ran for our vehicles to wait out the onslaught.

The truck rocked back and forth as the winds whipped by. The rain came down in sheets, and the passenger-side window leaked. I had confidence that the truck was stable, but it was tilting far enough that I was a little concerned. The storm passed after about 30 minutes, the sun flashed out from behind the clouds, and the technician arrived.

A simple change of a fuel filter fixed the problem and put us on the road again. We triumphantly pushed on the gas and powered the truck up to speed. As we entered the stretch of road where the thunderstorm had formed, we passed three overturned semitrucks. These massive cargo haulers looked like toy trucks that had been turned over by a mischievous toddler. They hadn't crashed. They hadn't driven off the road. They were just on their sides. It was pretty obvious that they had parked on the side of the road to ride out the storm, and the wind was the impish child that interrupted their lives. As we drove by, we all thought, *That could have been us. If we hadn't been frustrated by truck trouble, we would have arrived at the same time as these tractor trailers.*

I remember praying, "Jesus, I am sorry for complaining. Obviously, the trouble wasn't trouble at all. I don't want to make too big a deal out of this, but I'm really glad we were at that rest stop rather than on the road when that storm came through."

It felt like discipline when we were forced to wait, but it felt like love in the end.

He is awesome as a Savior. At some point in life, we come to the realization that we are not adequate in ourselves. We can do many things, but we can never earn eternal life. We all live with a nagging realization of our imperfections. During moments of honesty, we admit that we have a desperate need for a Savior who can save us from ourselves and our self-destructive tendencies. Jesus is that Savior.

I (Bill) grew up in a self-sufficient home. My dad is a talented engineer with an easy going temperament. He has never felt a deep need to know Jesus and has lived an exemplary life of integrity and honesty. My mom is an artistic, commanding woman. She likes only her ideas and manipulates all circumstances to get her way. Her need to control causes her to not trust people and to shrink down her life to a size she can keep under her authority.

My training taught me to be self-sufficient, but my soul told me something different. I had a nagging sense that things were not right in my life, but I could never pinpoint the problem. I lacked confidence and I was very hard on myself. I focused on the statements my mom made about my not having what it takes to be successful as I ignored evidence that I was intelligent and talented. I competed in school and sports, but I never could find it within myself to win a competition or perform at my potential. I was spectacularly mediocre…until I met Jesus.

Meeting Jesus at age 16 was the greatest interruption I have ever experienced. He gave me a love I never knew existed. My heart ignited with passion to know God. The Bible came alive. As I read, words jumped off the pages and changed the way I viewed myself. I began to grow in confidence as I believed what God said about me. I co-led with my brother a Bible study of 60 high school students before we ever had enough experience to have that kind of influence. I woke up early once a week to attend a prayer meeting before school even though waking early had always been hard for me.

I thought for a while that my youthful enthusiasm wouldn't have the stamina to last throughout adulthood, but it has been just the opposite. I have a life filled with experiences I would have been afraid of as a child. I have traveled to foreign countries, been on national TV, and interacted with highly influential people. I used to sweat profusely whenever I spoke in front of a crowd, but now I speak in front of crowds most weeks. I used to be afraid of people knowing about my life, and now I tell my story as often as I can if it will help people.

This is what Jesus does. He takes what wasn't working and transforms it into a life that honors Him and influences others.

He is the author of second chances. Walking with Jesus is vital because we all need second chances. We all wrestle with weaknesses and infirmities, and some of these we developed as we grew up. Every family has unhealthy dynamics in them so we all grow up in imperfect environments. We hope the unhealthy aspects of your home were minor and had little impact on you. But even if the unhealthy characteristics of your childhood were dramatic, they are not too big for Jesus. He is the greatest healer the world has ever known, and He can easily help you put them in perspective and grow. He can renew your mind, change your heart, bind your wounds, and help scar tissue replace the scabs and open wounds of your soul.

Some of the setbacks of your life are of your own doing. You may have made poor decisions or you may have lived recklessly for a while. You may have hurt other people or burned bridges that you wish you could now cross. The memory of what you've done haunts you and tries to convince you that Jesus has no real use for you. Nothing could be further from the truth.

The apostle Paul is the most influential writer of the New Testament, which is remarkable when you consider his past. By his own admission, he "was formerly a blasphemer and a persecutor and a violent aggressor" (1 Timothy 1:13). He even said of himself, "I am the least of the apostles and do not even deserve to be called an apostle, because I persecuted the church of God" (1 Corinthians 15:9). He was an ignorant enemy of Christ and the last person anyone would have thought could be a follower of Christ, let alone become the most significant Christian leader of his day. He never forgot his past mistakes, but he did not allow them to erase the power of the grace of God in his life.

The secret of his strength was in his acceptance of God's second chance. He had proved what he could be on his own and finally concluded, "by the grace of God I am what I am" (1 Corinthians 15:10). He received forgiveness and a new purpose. Jesus didn't erase the memory of his past, but He did fashion a powerful future.

Without Jesus, we are bound to figure out on our own how to recover from our mistakes. When we walk with Jesus, the grace of God that can heal, forgive, and transform becomes ours. It's a hard road, but just like Paul, we can embrace God's grace despite the pain of our past choices.

He adds adventure to life. Jesus has plans. He died for the sins of the whole world, and all who believe in Him are adopted into His family and granted an inheritance. He has sent ambassadors into the world, and He has planted His church to keep the message alive. He will one day return to earth to take over what is rightfully His. All who belong to Him will be given significant places of responsibility under His leadership. In the meantime, He leads us on an adventure that is worth everything we have to give.

Jesus is a big thinker, and He is always working on a big plan. He understands our limitations and allows for our humanity, but He never settles for less than He can accomplish through us. The Holy Spirit who resides in us is fully aware of what He can do and how much we are capable of with His help. He has equipped us to tear down strongholds, defeat evil, and take thoughts captive. We are warriors outfitted to do battle against everything that opposes the grace of God. Some of us serve as frontline soldiers, some of us serve as medics, and some of us serve as support personnel, but we all have a place that matters.

Most people settle for far too little. We are made to walk with Jesus, but we settle for relying on ourselves. We are made to overcome false thinking that distorts the message of salvation, but we settle for distractions that help us avoid thinking at all. We are empowered to live influential lives that help others grow stronger, but we settle for a selfish pursuit of more things. Jesus knows these are all temporary, so He challenges us to join Him in the adventure of redeeming the world to Himself.

You are an ambassador and you matter in God's plan. The best way to find your place in His adventure is to walk with Him.

Just for Fun

One day a group of eminent scientists got together and decided that mankind had come a long way and no longer needed God. So they picked one scientist to go and tell Him that they were done with Him.

The scientist walked up to God and said, "God, we've decided that we no longer need You. We're to the point that we can clone people and do many miraculous things, so why don't You just retire?"

God listened patiently to the man and then said, "Very well, but first, how about this: Let's have a man-making contest."

To which the scientist replied, "Okay, great!"

But God added, "Now, we're going to do this just like I did back in the old days with Adam."

The scientist said, "Sure, no problem" and bent down and grabbed himself a handful of dirt.

God looked at him and said, "No, no, no. You go get your own dirt!"[2]

CHAPTER 3

Decide to Celebrate

"The fruit of the Spirit is...joy."

GALATIANS 5:22

We were made to celebrate. If you take time to watch children, you'll see in them an insatiable drive to have a good time and find a reason to rejoice.

We were recently involved in a couple's wedding celebration. The night before, family and friends gathered to share stories and encourage this new couple. One of the stories involved a young boy. His mom said she was looking for a nanny to help out with her three very active, enthusiastic children. She posted an ad at the local Christian college and began scheduling interviews. The interview with the bride-to-be went well, but Mom remained cautious because she had other candidates to talk with. Her plan changed immediately, however, when her youngest son bolted to his feet, threw his fist in the air, and blurted out, "We have a winner!"

During the reception, the maid of honor stood to give a toast and said, "I am so excited for my sister today. I can still remember playing house together as little girls. Even though I was the younger sister, I always played the role of mother. So today I feel like my daughter is getting married!"

I (Bill) was amazed that a fully grown woman was still rejoicing over great memories from childhood. I shouldn't have been so astonished; this is the way we are. We imagine victories, we role play adventures, and we dream of exploits that bring fulfillment to our hearts. It started in us as kids, and it longs to continue throughout our adult lives. It's a challenge, however, because life is filled with complex problems and cranky people.

The apostle Paul calls us to celebrate in Philippians 4:4, "Rejoice in the Lord always. I will say it again: Rejoice!" He wants us to keep our hearts focused on the good things God is doing. He is not naïve, however, about the realities of life. In Galatians 5:19-21, he describes the source of what makes problems so complex and people so cranky, "The acts of the sinful nature are obvious: sexual immorality, impurity and debauchery; idolatry and witchcraft; hatred, discord, jealousy, fits of rage, selfish ambition, dissensions, factions and envy; drunkenness, orgies, and the like. I warn you, as I did before, that those who live like this will not inherit the kingdom of God."

We don't celebrate because life is easy and simple. We celebrate because the reason we have to rejoice is bigger than our troubles. The fact that troubles exist is obvious to all of us and is reflected in a plethora of pithy sayings. Here are just a few:

- "If you break your neck, if you have nothing to eat, if your house is on fire, then you got a problem. Everything else is inconvenience."—Robert Fulghum[1]

- "Pain is inevitable. Suffering is optional."—M. Kathleen Casey[2]

- "I know God will not give me anything I can't handle. I just wish that He didn't trust me so much."—Mother Teresa[3]

- "If I had a formula for bypassing trouble, I would not pass it round. Trouble creates a capacity to handle it. I don't embrace trouble; that's as bad as treating it as an enemy. But I do say meet it as a friend, for you'll see a lot of it and had better be on speaking terms with it."—Oliver Wendell Holmes[4]

- "If you can find a path with no obstacles, it probably doesn't lead anywhere."—Frank A. Clark[5]

- "The problem is not that there are problems. The problem is expecting otherwise and thinking that having problems is a problem."—Theodore Rubin[6]

- "God will not look you over for medals, degrees, or diplomas, but for scars."—Elbert Hubbard[7]

Our Decision to Choose Joy

I (Pam) know what it is to decide to celebrate life. As I speak to groups of women in my Seasoned Sisters ministry (www.seasonedsisters.com), I describe one of the most challenging times of our life.

If my life were described as a hand crocheted afghan, then one day someone grabbed one piece of thread of the afghan and began to unravel my life as I knew it.

Here's just a snapshot of time during what became a transition that lasted over four years. I was told by my doctor that I was four times more likely to have a heart attack than the average woman because of my family tree. She told me that I needed to make some key life changes or the second half of my life would not be very long.

Bill had been the picture of health and all of the sudden his blood pressure went through the roof. This got our attention because his grandfather died of a stroke at age 47 and his father had a stroke that left him paralyzed and disabled at age 48. Bill was 45. The super productive husband I had known was going to bed at 6:00 p.m. and still seemed exhausted the next day when he rose. The doctors were baffled by his erratic BP that would normalize then shoot up for no apparent reason.

At the time, Bill and I had achieved some measure of success as writers. One of our books had even hit the best-sellers list (*Men Are Like Waffles, Women Are Like Spaghetti*). Bill was also the senior pastor of the largest church in our city and we were completing a new building project. One day we were traveling, and Bill wasn't feeling well, so he went to the doctor. The doc asked about his life, "Got any stress?" When Bill described his mountain of responsibility, the physician replied, "Bill, you are a people helper. What would you tell someone who came into your office displaying these symptoms?"

Bill replied, "You have some strategic decisions to make and some life change is on the road ahead." *Exactly.* So to make a very long and painful story short, through a series of events and meetings, Bill ended up resigning from the church he'd pastored for over 15 years, a church where we loved the people and they loved us. It was the most difficult, emotionally draining, and painful experience either of us had ever survived. Mixed into the transition were all kinds of friendship and relational issues. The people closest to us fell into two groups: those who drew closer and offered emotional, spiritual, practical, and financial help, and those who didn't. Some just didn't know what to do, so they stayed away. Losing friends when you are already in emotional trauma only makes the trauma feel worse.

Initially, our anxiety level was through the roof. We both would go to bed every night and pray that, when we awoke, we'd be freed from this feeling of being dropped down the rabbit hole in *Alice in Wonderland.* We were in a bad dream and we wanted to wake up where everything was normal again. One of our best friends summarized our experience by saying, "It's like the dots just don't connect." We knew God would make a way for us, but we were looking frantically for the trailhead to get on the new path.

The anxiety and emotional pain was intense. At times, I felt as if I was going to have a heart attack. At night, when I placed my head on the pillow, it felt like someone was sitting on my chest. We had taught on midlife transitions (crisis), but now we were experiencing our own.

I was also desperate to do anything to regain my husband's health and somehow protect my own in the process. I was going to bed praying at night that Bill would be alive when I woke up next to him. I took on more of the financial earning responsibility so Bill could recover, rest, and regain his health. We continued to speak and write (and were amazingly successful at it despite all the transitions because God is a good and gracious God!). The pace was different than before. For a time, Bill was working half the hours he previously had, which isn't saying much since he often worked 90 hours per week before he was sick.

While we purposely slowed Bill's pace, I felt my own life stress and responsibility grow exponentially. You see, at the time of the life transition, all our sons were teens (at the time 13, 17, and 19). I was trying to keep one kid in college and prepare another for his college education, all during a time when there was a huge income shift. Prior to the health issues, we had poured what savings we had into charitable work, our children's education, and our business expansion. In addition, one company owed us the equivalent of six months of both our salaries. So with about half of the prior cash flow, we were supposed to maintain the same level of responsibilities and obligations. To say the least, the financial pressure was very real on both of us, despite the success we were experiencing in writing and speaking. In addition to our own lives, we had employees, whose families were depending on us at a time when we did not feel very dependable.

One week in particular sticks out to me as a picture of our life. Caleb (then 13) was hit illegally in a football game and had to be rushed to Children's Hospital. We discovered he had internal bleeding and had to have a blood transfusion. He was in ICU for the next eight days. I found myself sitting with Bill next to Caleb praying for both their lives to be spared. When we finally brought Caleb home, I had a speaking engagement that the family needed me to keep (because they kind of like groceries in the fridge). I left Caleb in Bill's wonderful care. The first night I was gone, our middle son, Zach, was pulled from his football game with a concussion and knee injury. The next night, our oldest, a junior college quarterback, was pulled from the game with what we thought might be a career-ending/scholarship-ending injury. When I landed at the airport, my sister-in-law was on the phone with the news that my 40-year-old brother had experienced a heart attack.

I prayed in desperation, *Lord, who am I supposed to save first?*

One day, while sitting with Caleb in ICU, I picked up a manuscript I was asked to endorse called *Gracepoints: Growth and Guidance During Times of Change* by my friend Jane Rubietta. There is a line in her book that will forever be tattooed onto my heart: "God is working just beyond the headlights of your life."

I am a pretty transparent person, so my feelings show on my face. Even if people didn't know the cause, they could easily pick up that I was experiencing stress. People cared, so they inquired. I just didn't know how to reply when people would ask, "So how are you doing?" The answer was either too long, too personal, or too depressing. I didn't want to wreck their day. Oftentimes when asked, "How are you doing?" We respond in an Eeyore kind of moan, "Well, pretty good under the circumstances." I love Professor Howard Hendricks's response, "Under the circumstances? What are you doing under there?"

I began to pray and ask God how to answer. God simply responded, "What kind of woman do you want to be, Pam?"

"Lord, I want to be the kind of person who can look at whatever life sends her way and find joy in it. Your Word says, 'The joy of the LORD is our strength,' and do I ever need strength right now! So I guess joy is the answer."

As a result, I changed my response to the question, "How are you doing?" My new answer became, "Choosin' joy!" (It helped even more when I would say it with a bit of attitude, so I'd fling up my hand like a cheerleader and shout with a smile, "Choosin' joy!")

And guess what? I found joy! It didn't come all at once, like a tidal wave. It was more like a small spring that began to bubble up. Precious, life-altering, and lifesaving joy!

The Big Reason

Just what is the big reason we have for rejoicing no matter the circumstances? It can be summed up in the phrase, "We are free!"

First of all, *we are free from condemnation* (Romans 8:1). On our own, we deserve to stand before God and be charged guilty for our actions and attitudes. Jesus wasn't satisfied to leave us in that state, however, so He gave His life so we might be free from the sentence of guilt. "So if the Son sets you free, you will be free indeed" (John 8:36).

We are also free from sin. This is one of those statements that's easy to say but much harder to explain. It isn't that we're free from ever making mistakes again. It's that we now have a fighting chance to do what is right. Once you meet Jesus, righteousness calls out to you just like sin used to call out to you. This is the point of Romans 6:22-23, "But now that you have been set free from sin and have become slaves to God, the benefit you reap leads to holiness, and the result is eternal life. For the wages of sin is death, but the gift of God is eternal life in Christ Jesus our Lord."

We used to be slaves to our lower nature. It had authority to order us around and make demands of us. Sin is a relentless master that constantly tells us what to do and nags us to join in unhealthy living. Now that we know Christ, we are free from sin's mastery. The Holy Spirit now relentlessly calls us to walk paths of blessing and do what is best. Our salvation is already settled, so our performance does not determine our eternal destiny. The beauty is that we now have the opportunity to choose what is right and, more often than not, succeed at doing what is healthy and productive. Without the freedom that comes from knowing Christ, people are shortsighted and intensely prone to choose self-destructive options.

Third, we are free to love. We're not talking about the weak kind of love that is simply intent on being nice to people. We're talking about the kind of love that changes people's lives. When you find true joy and realize that your eternity is set, you gain the freedom to help others find what is best for them. Paul saw this as a winning lifestyle:

> Though I am free and belong to no man, I make myself a slave to everyone, to win as many as possible…I have become all things to all men so that by all possible means I might save some…Do you not know that in a race all the runners run, but only one gets the prize? Run in such a way as to get the prize (1 Corinthians 9:19-24).

Part of this freedom is an ability to sacrifice for the sake of others. In 1 Corinthians 8:9, Paul challenges us to use our freedom to help those who have a weaker conscience. Rather than being a slave to selfishness, we can adjust our behavior so that others are benefited.

Alice took her children to a restaurant where her six-year-old son asked if he could say grace. "God is good. God is great. Thank You for the food, and I would thank You even more if Mom gets us ice cream for dessert. And liberty and justice for all! Amen!"

Along with the laughter from the other customers nearby, a woman remarked, "That's what's wrong with this country. Kids today don't even know how to pray. Asking God for ice cream! Why, I never!"

Hearing this, the boy burst into tears and asked, "Did I do it wrong? Is God mad at me?"

As Alice held him and assured him that he had done a terrific job, an elderly gentleman approached the table. He winked and said, "I happen to know that God thought that was a great prayer."

"Really?"

"Cross my heart," the man replied. Then in a theatrical whisper he added (indicating the woman whose remark had started this whole thing), "Too bad she never asks God for ice cream. A little ice cream is good for the soul sometimes."

Naturally, they had ice cream at the end of the meal. The little boy stared at his for a moment, then picked up his sundae and, without a word, placed it in front of the woman.

With a big smile he told her, "Here, this is for you. Ice cream is good for the soul sometimes; and my soul is good already."[8]

One of the greatest freedoms is the liberty to make decisions. The freedom comes from the Spirit who lives in us, and He gives us new wisdom. We can actually think God's thoughts when it comes to the choices we make because we have been given the mind of Christ. We don't want to say that we can think as clearly or comprehensively as God Himself, but the Bible is clear that He shares with us His wisdom as part of our freedom in Christ (1 Corinthians 2:10-16). Because we have the freedom to choose, we are called to follow the directions of Jesus. These are given in principle and demonstrated by example.

- "May the God who gives endurance and encouragement give you a spirit of unity among yourselves as you follow Christ Jesus" (Romans 15:5).

- "Follow my example, as I follow the example of Christ" (1 Corinthians 11:1).

- "Follow the way of love and eagerly desire spiritual gifts" (1 Corinthians 14:1).

This freedom to choose is good news because, remember, joy is a decision of the heart to celebrate life in good times, bad times, and boring times. So, what are the decisions that help us keep joy alive?

Celebrate Integrity

All relationships are easier when they are genuine, and the greatest stealer of joy in life is a relationship in turmoil.

I (Bill) was sitting in a seminar one day listening to a prominent leader when he had a staggering moment of disclosure. He said to us, "As you lead, be very aware of the 'joy suckers.' These are people who are determined to suck the joy out of everything they are involved with. In fact, I have noticed there is great rejoicing in organizations when there is a funeral for a 'joy sucker.'"

I almost fell off my seat when I heard him say it. I agreed with what he said; I just never thought someone would say it out loud!

I believe the main reason there is so much trauma in relationships is that people lack integrity. They make verbal commitments but don't have the resolve to follow through with them. They say they will sacrifice but quickly decide it's too hard and that too much is being asked. People convince others they are loyal and committed to the same goals, but then they manipulate circumstances to take over while they move others out of the way. People gossip when they should be friends. They criticize when they should be supportive. They lie when they should be honest.

As a result, most of us have stories of friendships, work relationships, and church conflicts that have surprised us and broken our hearts. Being able to look yourself in the eye, knowing that you've treated people well, is much better.

Have you ever avoided someone because you owed them money? Have you stayed home from a function because you have previously yelled at someone who was going to be there or gossiped about them to others? Have you disintegrated friendships because you mistreated others to fulfill your own selfish agenda? That can really curtail your social life! If you have to figure out how to avoid people because you haven't been living in accordance with how God would treat others, life can get complicated in a hurry. We don't have to contribute to this kind of interaction.

Relationships can feel complicated at times, especially if the other person is not living in accord with how God would treat people. Josh McDowell developed a simple way to help us all live with integrity in our relationships. He put three question marks on a set of dog tags for his son and a heart formed out of three question marks on a necklace for his daughter. What are the three question marks for, you ask? They are a reminder to ask three questions that maintain JOY in any and all relationships:

Does your decision or action show respect for **J**esus?
Does your decision or action show respect for **O**thers?
Does your decision or action show respect for **Y**ourself?

We have seen that people who pause to ask these questions before they say or do things are better able to stay under the umbrella of God's blessing. Their friendships have fewer issues, their business network is more effective, and their influence on others is more trusted.

Celebrate the Blessing

Recently I (Pam) was walking from a convention center back to my hotel. It was just an eight-block evening stroll, and I was looking forward to the relaxed walk with my friend. However, four blocks from the hotel the sky opened up and dumped buckets of rain. We tried to run, but the path was slippery. We looked desperately for overhangs and awnings to no avail. We arrived at the hotel soaking wet and looking anything but professional. We could have changed everything had we just been under an umbrella.

Life is the same. Life is hard and imperfect. Because of the fall and sin, storms come our way that interrupt our lives and challenge our attitudes. However, when we're under the umbrella of God's blessing, we don't add to the downpour of trials with more consequences of our own bad choices. Integrity spares us from ourselves. Walking in God's ways, in a sense, protects or shelters us from much of life's hardships because God promises to watch over those whose hearts are His. Even the extreme examples of a Job or a Jeremiah, who teach us how to deal with suffering and hardships, demonstrate that God's presence and provision carried them through very tough circumstances. God's faithfulness helped each of them maintain attitudes and inward choices that served as a rudder amidst the storm.

> For the eyes of the LORD range throughout the earth to strengthen those whose hearts are fully committed to him (2 Chronicles 16:9).

> But without faith it is impossible to please God, because anyone who comes to him must believe that he exists and that he rewards those who earnestly seek him (Hebrews 11:6).

God looks for ways to bless us, so what does it mean to be blessed? There are two distinct ideas behind the word *blessing* in the Bible. The first carries the idea "to speak well of another person" or "to provide with power for success or prosperity." A couple of examples are:

Praise [Blessed] be to the God and Father of our Lord Jesus Christ, who has *blessed* us in the heavenly realms with every spiritual blessing in Christ (Ephesians 1:3).

Do not repay evil with evil or insult with insult, but with *blessing*, because to this you were called so that you may inherit a *blessing* (1 Peter 3:9).

The second idea behind *blessing* is the notion of happiness. It is common for people in the modern world to think of happiness as feeling good about yourself and your life. This is certainly *the result* of what the Bible refers to as happiness, but it's not the primary idea. The primary focus of happiness in the Old Testament refers to the material goods God brings to a person's life in response to his decisions to live correctly. Being blessed was evidenced by material wealth and vocational advancement. It might have included many kids, abundant crops or flocks, riches, beauty, good health, monetary wealth, social standing, or respect in the community. We, therefore, read statements such as these:

Blessed is the man
    who does not walk in the counsel of the wicked
or stand in the way of sinners
    or sit in the seat of mockers.
But his delight is in the law of the Lord,
    and on his law he meditates day and night.
He is like a tree planted by streams of water,
    which yields its fruit in season
and whose leaf does not wither.
    Whatever he does prospers.
      (Psalm 1:1-3)

In the New Testament, the idea of blessing or happiness still revolves around God's provision, but it takes on a long-term view. Grace gives us salvation that provides eternal stability and prosperity. Because we live in the midst of a spiritual war, we may not experience the abundance here on earth if we follow Christ. When we enter the presence of Christ, however, we will have all we need and more. It is certain because of the death and resurrection of Christ.

Happiness then is the conviction that my life has been taken care of in abundance for eternity, which gives my life honor, respect, confidence, and stability. This is the message of the Beatitudes in Jesus' Sermon on the Mount in Matthew 5:

> Now when he saw the crowds, he went up on a mountainside and sat down. His disciples came to him, and he began to teach them, saying:
>
> "Blessed are the poor in spirit,
>   for theirs is the kingdom of heaven.
> Blessed are those who mourn,
>   for they will be comforted.
> Blessed are the meek,
>   for they will inherit the earth.
> Blessed are those who hunger and thirst for righteousness,
>   for they will be filled.
> Blessed are the merciful,
>   for they will be shown mercy.
> Blessed are the pure in heart,
>   for they will see God.
> Blessed are the peacemakers,
>   for they will be called sons of God.
> Blessed are those who are persecuted
>   because of righteousness,
>   for theirs is the kingdom of heaven.
> "Blessed are you when people insult you, persecute you and falsely say all kinds of evil against you because of me. Rejoice and be glad, because great is your reward in heaven, for in the same way they persecuted the prophets who were before you."
>   (vv. 1-12)

Many of the circumstances mentioned are not good or pleasant, but they bring happiness or blessedness because they are evidence that we will be with Jesus. We will eventually have everything we need and so much more that we won't know what to do with it all.

Being blessed or happy, then, means that you have discovered a relationship with God and you are confident you will be fully rewarded when the time is right.

Pastor John Hagee shares a story that illustrates the attitude that develops when you choose to celebrate the blessing regardless of your circumstances:

> There was a widow living in a small apartment with her two children. She was struggling to survive and support her children. The landlord was a mean and cruel man who proclaimed himself an atheist. He continually raised the rent, generally making life as difficult as possible for this God-fearing Christian widow. One morning the evil landlord was outside the widow's apartment and heard her praying to God for the blessing of some food and supplies that she might feed her children. So, the landlord ran to the grocery store and bought up several bags of food and other supplies. He put all the bags on her doorstep, knocked on her door and then quickly hid in the bushes nearby.
>
> The widow opened the door and saw the bags of food and supplies. She rejoiced, calling the children, and praising the Lord! She continued to shout, "Glory to God!"
>
> The evil landlord came from the bushes, saying, "Old woman, God didn't bring those bags. You're crazy! I heard you praying and went and got the stuff just to show you how crazy you are praying."
>
> The widow began to shout even louder, praising God and dancing about.
>
> The landlord yelled, "Crazy woman, didn't you hear me! What are so happy about?"
>
> The widow smiled and said, "Not only did God buy me the supplies, but He got the Devil to deliver it!"[9]

Celebrate Your Potential, Corral Your Dark Side

God created you with remarkable potential. You influence others by your character, your conversations, your career, and your commitments. As a result, you should be celebrated. Part of living with joy involves seeking to maximize the potential that resides in your soul. Only you can fulfill God's plan for your life. If you are excited about that, you will work hard, adjust your commitments regularly, and seek training to get better.

The problem is that our ability to mess up our lives grows along with the ability to expand our influence. As a result, we see talented, effective people who seemingly out of nowhere make poor decisions that trash their lives.

- Why would President Clinton risk so much for sexual encounters with intern Monica Lewinsky?
- Why would Tiger Woods risk his billions and his marriage and family for sex with multiple women?
- How could John Edwards risk his shot at the presidency for a fling while his wife suffered with cancer?
- Why would Lindsay Lohan and Britney Spears self-destruct before our eyes at the peak of their success?
- How could Ted Haggard, a pastor of a megachurch and president of the National Association of Evangelicals, risk a stable marriage and family to have a liaison with a homosexual masseuse?

They all did these things because they are like us—they each had a dark side. As their confidence grew, their ability to make big mistakes grew. Sam Rima and Gary McIntosh, in their book *Overcoming the Dark Side of Leadership,*[10] give us a wakeup call as they remind us that we *all* have a dark side. They skillfully describe the importance of allowing God to redeem the hurts of our lives and fortify us with His love so that we do not give in to the leanings of the dark side of our souls.

> It was during this research that it became clear that a paradox of sorts existed in the lives of most of the leaders who had experienced significant failures: The personal insecurities, feelings of inferiority, and need for parental approval (among other dysfunctions) that compelled these people to become successful leaders were very often the same issues that precipitated their failure.[11]

None of us has had a perfect journey, so God combines the success and setbacks of our lives into a package that impacts the world. He starts with our God-given personality and giftedness and, if we are willing, He redeems our inferiorities, mistakes, and hurts to shape us into the people He wants us to be. These are powerful forces in our lives, so they create ambition which must be managed well.

> Most often their ambition has been a subtle and dangerous combination of their own dysfunctional personal needs and a certain measure of their altruistic desire to expand the kingdom of God. However, because ambition is so easily disguised in Christian circles and couched in spiritual language (the need to fulfill the Great Commission and expand the church), the dysfunctions that drive Christian leaders often go undetected and unchallenged until it is too late.[12]

As Rima and MacIntosh expose us to the reality of the dark side in each of us, they give us a framework to help us identify how it manifests itself in us. We have taken their insightful framework of "darkside" motivations and have added other observations from our over 30 years in relationship ministry. All of us have tendencies toward unhealthy behavior, and each of us has a particular propensity toward one of the following behavior patterns:

Compulsive: A person who is status conscious, is in authority or looks for approval from authority, leans toward controlling behaviors and is often a workaholic. Outward productivity and approval reassure them and help life feel more in control. This person can also be moralistic or judgmental. Deep down he feels life is out of control so he must control it.

Narcissistic: A person who truly believes life revolves around her and her needs. She is driven to succeed by a need for admiration or acclaim. She has an overly inflated sense of importance as well as great ambitions and grandiose fantasies and ideas. Deep down she feels insecure and inferior, so she needs to build herself up.

Paranoid: A person whose fears stop him from living a normal life. He is suspicious, jealous, fearful, and hypersensitive of the actions of others. He fears others might do something to unravel his life and leadership. He attaches subjective meanings to others' motives and can create rigid structures to maintain control of situations or people. Deep down he is afraid of life and love.

Codependent: A person who seeks approval from a toxic person or lives life "around" another's needs and desires to the detriment of her own life or needs. She will seem like a peacemaker just because she does not want to confront real issues but would rather cover them up. She takes on others' work and burdens and can have too high a tolerance for sin in others. Deep down, codependent people are repressed and frustrated because they never speak up or speak out their true feelings or thoughts.

Passive-Aggressive: A person who establishes one expectation then does the opposite. He is stubborn, intentionally inefficient, lazy, or forgetful. He complains, resists, and procrastinates as a means of controlling others around him. He can also occasionally use a small burst of depression or anger to control. Deep down, he is angry and bitter. He might fear success as others raise expectations on him and push him to perform.

We encourage everyone to take the "dark-side" test in Rima and McIntosh's book for a more accurate, specific inventory of what might snag your life. Then develop a plan that will diminish the influence of your dark side as you expand the positive impact of your life.

Personal Profile

Try it. Select which "dark side" trait you are most susceptible to and note the trait of God you should focus on to battle this weakness:

My Dark Side	God's Light
Compulsive	God's freedom, grace, mercy
Narcissistic	God as King, Ruler, Lord
Paranoid	God's provision, protection, peace
Codependent	God dependence, God pleaser, serving God
Passive-Aggressive	God's path and plan as priority

I believe my dark-side weakness might be _____

One thing I can do to address this weakness is: _____

Ken Johnson, the chaplain of the Super Bowl champion Indianapolis

Colts, is famous for saying, "Don't get stuck on stupid," and "Let your character keep you where your talent can take you." The more you allow God to redeem your dark side, the more freedom you experience. The more freedom you experience, the more celebrating you will do.

The man who epitomizes for me (Bill) the commitment to celebrate life regardless of what life brings your way is Jim Valvano. He was the head basketball coach for North Carolina State in 1983 when they unexpectedly won the NCAA National Championship. In 1992, at the age of 46, he was diagnosed with terminal cancer, which took his life in 1993. His positive attitude and infectious inspiration led to the development of the V Foundation for Cancer Research.[13] The words he spoke after finding out about his unwanted gift have continued to be an inspiration to anyone who wants to rejoice as a lifestyle:

> To me, there are three things we all should do every day. We should do this every day of our lives. Number one is laugh. You should laugh every day. Number two is think. You should spend some time in thought. And number three is, you should have your emotions moved to tears, could be happiness or joy. But think about it. If you laugh, you think, and you cry, that's a full day. That's a heck of a day. You do that seven days a week, you're going to have something special.[14]

The apostle Paul put it succinctly and emphatically when he told the church at Philippi, "Rejoice in the Lord always. I will say it again: Rejoice!" (Philippians 4:4).

Just for Fun

We are all grateful for the following development, but we imagine the main character in this true story struggled to celebrate his contribution to the world:

> Captain Edward A. Murphy Jr. was an engineer with the U.S. Air Force in 1949 when he created the harness for a rocket-powered sled designed to move faster than a speeding bullet, testing how much acceleration and deceleration a human being could tolerate. The test failed, and the sled's passenger

(Major John Paul Stapp) was temporarily blinded because—as Murphy later discovered—every one of the harness's gauges had been installed backward.

Exasperated, Murphy made a snide comment that if there were two ways to do something and one could result in catastrophe, someone would invariably choose to do it the catastrophic way. His colleagues overheard him and began repeating the adage. Before long, "Murphy's Law" caught on and became widely quoted. It was added to *Webster's Dictionary* in 1958.[15]

CHAPTER 4

Decide to Live in Peace

"The fruit of the Spirit is…peace."

GALATIANS 5:22

The Toyota Prius has become popular as a hybrid car that switches from electricity to petroleum to drive the wheels. In a similar way, you are a sophisticated creation made up of many "systems" that interact to produce energy, focus, and motivation. As you become familiar with the way you are wired, and have several tools to make the best use of your unique crafting by God's hand, your life will be more productive. This chapter introduces several tools or systems for self-discovery and awareness.

When these systems are functioning properly, your life runs smoothly with plenty of oomph and wisdom. When any of these systems malfunction or are misapplied, life becomes strenuous or ineffective. When the alarms sound telling you that something is off, you need to have a clear understanding of your God-given makeup in order to adjust your life and get it back in operating order.

The systems that make your life run at peak performance are both simple and profound. They are simple enough that you can apply the information immediately. At the same time, they are profound enough that you can spend the rest of your life and invest an enormous amount of resources studying the intricacies of how they work. This chapter is the simple, user-friendly version, but we have included in the endnotes a list of resources if you want to explore any of these further.

The Bible reminds us that we are "fearfully and wonderfully made"

(Psalm 139:14). The prophet Jeremiah was reminded that his purpose and plan were designed by God before his birth:

> "Before I formed you in the womb I knew you,
>> before you were born I set you apart;
>>> I appointed you as a prophet to the nations."
>>> (Jeremiah 1:5)

And in the Book of Proverbs, parents are reassured:

> Train up a child in the way he should go;
>> even when he is old he will not depart from it.
>> (Proverbs 22:6 ESV)

The phrase "the way he should go" can also be translated "according to his or her God-given bent." Each of us has unique God-given tendencies. We were wired a certain way to give ultimate glory to God with our lives. First Corinthians 6:20 and 10:31 remind us that God has invested heavily for the opportunity to fulfill His plan in us. "You were bought at a price. Therefore honor God with your body...So whether you eat or drink or whatever you do, do it all for the glory of God." The early church father Irenaeus echoed this thought when he wrote, "The glory of God is man fully alive."

Designed to Glorify

The goal then is to be fully alive in a way that is at peace with the way God designed you. You will increase your ability to succeed as you lower your stress. Peace will guard your heart as you live in congruence and harmony with the way you were created. People don't get distressed because they do too much. They get distressed because they do too much of what they weren't designed to do. When you live in a way that is not really who you are, you are more prone to other people's expectations and the fear of failure. We all have to function in many different settings, but if you can do so with the way you operate best, life will be less stressful, more productive, and definitely more enjoyable.

Motivational Styles

Life requires a lot of energy because work and relationships place constant demands on our time and talents. When these demands line up with your natural motivation, stress remains at appropriate levels and your effectiveness is maximized. But when you are not naturally motivated to meet these demands, stress rises and your effectiveness diminishes. The more you operate in your natural motivational style, the more satisfied you will be with your relationships and with life in general. Natural motivational styles include:

- Temperament style
- Conflict-resolution style
- Learning style
- Love language
- Birth order
- Relax and recharge style
- Spiritual gifts
- Financial style
- Parenting style

Let's look at each of these styles a little closer.

Temperament Style

Your temperament determines the way you process the information of life. You discover your temperament by asking two strategic questions: "Am I more extroverted or introverted?" and "Am I more people-oriented or task-oriented?"

Introverts look at life from the inside out. They ask questions such as, "Do I feel emotionally connected to you?" "Does this career make me feel fulfilled?" "Do I feel close to God?" Introverts think before they speak. Sometimes they think long and hard.

Extroverts look at life from the outside in. They ask, "Am I spending enough time at work to climb the ladder?" "Am I spending enough time on my priorities?" "Am I doing the things that will build my relationships?" Extroverts tend to share whatever comes across their mind; they think out loud.

Which are you? Do you look at life from the outside in (extrovert) or from the inside out (introvert)?

Task-oriented individuals are very good at getting things done. Given the opportunity to spend time with people or finish a task, they will work on the task at hand with the thought, *Everyone will be better off when we get this done.*

People-oriented individuals are very good at spending time with others. They can get things done, but they are easily distracted when others are around because they sincerely want to know what is going on with these people. They firmly believe that *everything will get done when everyone is getting along.*

Which are you? Are you more task-oriented or people-oriented?

Combining the answers to these two questions provides four basic temperament types as seen in the following chart.

	Powerful	**Popular**	
	Decisive	Fun	
	Natural Leader	Spontaneous	
	Confident	Emotional	
	Entrepreneurial	Exciting	
	Self-starter	Caring	
Motivated by:	Visionary	Optimistic	**Motivated by:**
Control		Forgiving	**Attention**
	Perfect	**Peaceful**	
	Organized	Loyal	
	Efficient	Peacemaker	
	Attentive to detail	Easy going	
	High integrity	Flexible	
	Creative	Amiable	**Motivated by:**
	Detailed	Hard working	**Respect**
Motivated by:		"Vice president" role	
Control		Merciful	

Extroverts / Introverts

Task-Oriented ——— People-Oriented

An ancient Greek philosopher used the terms *sanguine, choleric, melancholy,* and *phlegmatic* to identify these four temperaments. In the notes at the back of this book, we have listed several resources for each personality type. We encourage you to study one of the many resources listed and, if you are a parent, have each member of your family take the fun temperament quizzes to discern his or her personality type. We will base our discussion on some easy-to-remember terms used by Florence Littauer, and we will add in what motivates each temperament:

- *Powerful* (choleric)—motivated by control of decisions; extroverted/task-oriented
- *Popular* (sanguine)—motivated by people time; extroverted/people-oriented
- *Peaceful* (phlegmatic)—motivated by peace and making peace; introverted/people-oriented
- *Perfect* (melancholy)—motivated by process and order; introverted/task-oriented

When you take a personality profile as an adult, try to think back to what you were like as a child of seven or eight. We adults have often learned to mask our true self in order to please other people. Or more positively, we have gained the skills to strengthen our perceived weaknesses with a goal of becoming more like Jesus. (Jesus would, of course, have all the strengths of all the personalities and none of the weaknesses.)

The Powerful

Cholerics are extroverted, task-oriented decision-makers and natural leaders. Bob Phillips labels them "drivers" and the DISC test uses the word "dominant." Gary Smalley and John Trent refer to them as "lions" because they love to be in charge. Their primary shortcomings are a lack of empathy and a bulldozer mentality. They are so focused on the task at hand, they can sometimes run over people to get it done. They are primarily motivated by control of the decisions that directly affect their lives. Fun to them is anything they decide on.

The best way to motivate a choleric is to give him or her choices. This powerful personality loves to be the leader or boss. Without these powerful personalities, the world might just stop because they are the driving force behind most great goals and dreams. Other people may dream great dreams, but cholerics wake up and make them happen.

Powerful personalities desire a cooperative environment, which means they create the environment—and you cooperate with it! A sign on their desk might read: *I'm not bossy, my ideas are just better.*

Traits of the Powerful Temperament that people love:

- Decisive
- Natural leader
- Confident
- Entrepreneurial
- Self-starter
- Visionary

Traits of the Powerful Temperament that people get frustrated with:

- Pushy
- Driven
- Short-tempered
- Egocentric

Kids with this personality might say things like:

> "Take risks. I mean, if you like this person and you don't know if they like you, ask them out and see what happens. I liked this girl and I asked her out. She said no and she hates me now, but I took that risk" (Bruce, age 13).

> "Once I'm done with kindergarten, I'm going to find me a wife" (Tom, 5).

> "Don't forget your wife's name. That will mess up the love" (Roger, 8).

Notice how direct they are? They love to live decisively!

The Popular

The other extrovert is the people-oriented sanguine. Smalley and Trent label these people "otters" because they love to have fun. Phillips calls them "expressive," and the DISC "inspirational." They are creative, spontaneous, and have super people skills. Their primary weakness is a lack of perseverance. (If it isn't fun, why stay at it?) They love a party, so they can seem shallow and flippant to some of the other personalities.

They are primarily motivated by people and praise. All they want is a little attention—okay, a lot of attention—and they will do anything to get it. If you want to motivate a sanguine, hook a task to a person or make it a party, and they are there for you. Without these popular personalities, many of us would have fewer friends. The popular personalities make the world a tolerable, happy place to dwell.

Traits of the Popular Temperament that people love:

- Fun
- Spontaneous
- Emotional
- Exciting
- Caring
- Optimistic
- Forgiving

Traits of the Popular Temperament that frustrate people:

- Flaky
- Unorganized
- Lack long-term focus
- Not serious enough

Kids with this personality might say things like:

> "A realist is more correct about things in life than an optimist. But the optimist seems to have more friends and much more fun" (Megan, age 14).

> "If you want to be loved by somebody who isn't already in your family, it doesn't hurt to be beautiful" (Jeanne, 8).

> "It isn't always just how you look. Look at me. I'm handsome

like anything and I haven't got anybody to marry me yet" (Gary, 7).

"Lovers will just be staring at each other and their food will get cold. Other people care more about the food" (Brad, 8).

"It's love if they order one of those desserts that are on fire. They like to order those because it's just like how their hearts are… on fire" (Christine, 9).

Notice how fun and friendly they are? Their lives are lived with flair!

THE PEACEFUL

The phlegmatic (Smalley and Trent's "golden retriever") is an introverted, amiable, steady, no-frills, peace-at-all costs, likable guy or gal. Phillips labels these as "amiable"; the DISC says they are "steady." Everybody loves the peaceful personality. Everyone gets along with them because their goal in life is not to rock the boat. Everyone likes the golden retriever unless you want something done, you need a decision out of them, or you are in a hurry. Then they can drive you crazy!

The theme song of the peaceful personality would be Otis Redding's "Respect." All they want is a little respect. When you show appreciation and respect to the phlegmatic, they will do almost anything for you. They might take a while, but they will get it done. Most of us just couldn't get along without these natural mediators.

Traits of the Peaceful Temperament that people love:

- Loyal

- Peacemaker

- Easygoing

- Flexible

- Amiable

- Hard working

- "Vice president" role

- Merciful

Traits of the Peaceful Temperament that frustrate people:

- Can lack intensity
- Coach-potato mentality
- Lack direction
- Can seem passive-aggressive

Kids with this personality might say things like:

> "Don't think life is easy, because when you get older it is hard work. I used to think life was easy, now I have to do the dishes every other day" (Nick, age 9).

> "Eighty-four is a good age to get married because you don't have to work anymore and you can spend all your time loving each other in your bedroom" (Judy, 8).

The Perfect

The melancholy personality is introverted and task-oriented. Most great artists and musicians are this personality. They are creative, and they want things done right. They have the patience to do things with excellence. Their perfectionism can drive other people, primarily the sanguine, crazy. The sanguine's response to a melancholy will always be "lighten up!" But they can't lighten up. The world is black and white and in desperate need of fixing. They can become negative and depressed because they see the glass half-empty, and they notice all the little undone things in the world.

The Smalley-Trent model calls these people "beavers" because they are hardworking and get the job done. The DISC test calls them "cautious," and Bob Phillips labels them "analytical." They are always thinking, always processing.

So make very few promises to your friends with this personality or you will lose credibility. If you say you are going to meet at 6:00 p.m., you'd better do it. If you come in at 6:20, you weren't just late—you lied. The perfect personality takes most things literally. Without the perfect personality, the world would be filled with so many more mistakes. Traffic lights wouldn't be synchronized. Chaos would happen without them!

Traits of the Perfect Temperament that people love:

- Organized
- Efficient
- Attentive to detail
- High integrity
- Creative
- Detailed in pursuits (music, health care, engineering, computer programming, editing)

Traits of the Perfect Temperament that frustrate people:

- Rigid
- Unforgiving
- Stubborn
- Negative

Kids with this personality might say things like:

"Never give up because life gets harder as you get older. After preschool the road of life keeps getting bumpier and bumpier and bumpier" (Angela, age 11).

"On the first date most people just tell each other lies, and that usually gets them interested enough to go for a second date" (Mike, 10).

"You should never kiss a girl unless you have enough bucks to buy her a big ring and her own DVD player 'cause she'll want to have videos of the wedding" (Jim, 10).

"To fall in love, I think you're supposed to get shot with an arrow or something, but the rest of it isn't supposed to be so painful" (Harlan, 8).

"One of you should know how to write a check. Because even if you have tons of love, there is still going to be a lot of bills" (Ava, 8).

"People in love hold hands because they want to make sure their rings don't fall off because they paid good money for them" (Dave, 8).

Notice they are practical and can be a little cynical, but they are attentive to details!

Personality Types and Relationships

We tend to make friends with those who have a temperament similar to our own, we are romantically attracted to people who have the opposite temperament, and vocationally we grow best in environments where all four temperaments are represented.

Since I (Pam) am sanguine and choleric, I can create ideas in bucketfuls, and I think all of them are brilliant, of course, just because I came up with them. I want to set sail with a host of ideas. I am most comfortable around friends who love ideas and love a fast pace. We get moving in conversation at record speeds and come up with more ways to change the world in an afternoon than most people can in a lifetime. We know we won't carry out most of these ideas, but the exploration is exhilarating.

In romance it is a completely different story. I was attracted to Bill, who is primarily peaceful with a "perfect" secondary temperament. He frustrates me at times with his cautious approach, but I recognize he is better at setting processes in place, helping me to sort through the ideas, and helping them rise to the level of excellence. I also recognize that I am calmer when I'm around him, but if I had to live at his pace every day, I would grow restless. When he is not around, I am more socially active, but I have to be more diligent to avoid making impetuous mistakes—possibly a few tragic ones.

Think about it—you will be more effective when you include people in your life who have other skills, gifts, traits, and motivations than you have so that together you can create a well-rounded, powerful team.

Some singles err here because those with opposite personalities can drive you crazy! Sometimes differences are perceived as weaknesses, so singles walk away from the very people who might best improve their lives simply because they are so different. Embrace friends who react to life differently than you do.

As a boss, I (Pam) do not need more people with lots of new ideas, because I have plenty for my team to work on. Instead, I need colleagues who are "perfect" to ensure things are done well and right, "popular" to ensure people are well taken care of en route, and "peaceful" to quietly serve and build loyal teams.

So who are you? How did God wire you?

Your Temperament Profile [1]

My primary temperament is: ☐ Popular ☐ Powerful
                             ☐ Peaceful ☐ Perfect

My secondary temperament is: ☐ Popular ☐ Powerful
                              ☐ Peaceful ☐ Perfect

My best trait is _____.

A negative trait I should work on is _____.

In my circle of influence, I need a few more of this personality style: _____.

In my dating life, I should consider dating my opposite, which is a _____.

(The *Wired That Way* test by Marita and Florence Littauer gives you an empirically sound look at yourself. This can be ordered at www.pamandbill.org under "Products.")

Conflict-Resolution Style

Dave and Claudia Arp have an easy way for people to picture the way they handle conflict. In the middle of interpersonal disagreements, which animal is most like the way you react? Are you a:

Turtle that withdraws? Turtles pull their head into their shell when they sense danger. You might walk out of the room when an argument breaks out or you might simply shut down emotionally and disengage.

Skunk that attacks? When you feel threatened do you attack back? Do you use sarcasm, put-downs, or more hostile tactics to force your own way?

Chameleon that yields? Do you change your opinions just to avoid discussion or drama? The chameleon has a danger of shoving stuff down, letting issues pile up and pile up. Then he will bolt and run, never to be heard from again, when he feels he "just can't take it anymore."

Owl that intellectualizes? When things get tough in a relationship, you wall off your feelings. You might share principles or give your advice or opinion, but your sentences would rarely begin with, "What I am feeling here is…"

Gorilla that must win at all costs? You will pull out all stops to win: manipulation, intimidation, or physical force. You carry grudges and keep notes on past offenses so you can use them later. You rarely say, "I'm sorry."[2]

It is helpful to know where you typically start when you feel hurt, betrayed, or attacked in a relationship. By knowing your default setting, you can address it immediately, or at least adjust your response quickly.

I (Pam) am a skunk by nature, so my natural tendency is to snap back and attack if I think I might fail or if someone makes an accusation against me. But I want to be more like Jesus, so I have preplanned responses that are calmer and kinder. I practice these responses for use when I am feeling like I want to spray negativity back to someone who is hurting me.

I (Bill) am a turtle who can easily withdraw from conversations. I decided early on that, when I feel like retreating, I should lean into the conflict and seek resolution and ask questions to gain understanding.

Your Conflict-Resolution Profile[3]

I am a _____ in conflict, so one thing that might help calm things down would be to _____.

Learning Style

In *The Way They Learn,* Cynthia Tobias, an educator, describes how people process information:

Auditory learners are those who remember information best if they hear it.

Visual learners are those who remember best if they have seen the information.

Kinesthetic learners are those who learn by experience or touch.

If you are out of school, you might think this isn't important. But consider how you best take in information to make a solid decision or learn new ideas to enhance your life. Some of you might need charts, others might need books on tape, and still others might need to walk through or experience the choices.

Your Learning Profile[4]

I learn best by (check one):   ☐ hearing   ☐ seeing
                                 ☐ doing

Your Love Language

We highly recommend Gary Chapman's *Five Love Languages*. All the expressions of love listed below can be effective, but each of us has a favorite way to receive love from our love interests, friends, and family. If you had to choose, which would be your favorite way to receive expressions of love?

> *Words of affirmation—when people say nice things*
>
> *Physical touch—when people give you a hug or pat on the back*
>
> *Quality time—when people spend time with you*
>
> *Acts of service—when people are willing to do favors for you*
>
> *Gifts—when people give you things (inexpensive or costly)*

A word of caution: If you are dating someone and you both prefer to receive love through physical touch, beware! Staying sexually pure might become an issue. You should also know each other's secondary love language so you can emphasize giving love in this manner while you are dating.

If you are dating someone and you want to figure out their love language, here are a couple of suggestions:

1. *Listen and look.* Do they repeat compliments others have made? Do they show you gifts they've been given? Do they tell you how a friend spent the day with them or how they came through for them in a pinch? Or do they hug everyone they meet?

2. *Try and test.* Use each love language with the person you are interested in and watch for their response. Offer a compliment, give a hug or pat on the back, spend uninterrupted time together just to listen, bail them out with a favor of service, give a well-thought-out gift. Which language got the best response? Which did they tell others about?

Knowing other people's love language is also a fun family activity. At a family gathering, give a love language test (it's in the back of Chapman's book). My sons know I (Pam) rank acts of service, then words of affirmation as my top two. This saves them a lot of money! If they give me "words that will make me cry" for Christmas or my birthday, it's a home run. But acts of service is my top love language, and this one is not as easy to fulfill. It often comes up when I need to be bailed out of a tough situation, or I need some manual labor for a move or an event.

Once, I introduced my son Brock to some of my friends who had recently heard me speak. They said, "It must be fun to have Pam for your mom. She is so hilarious!" Brock gave them a puzzled look and said, "Funny? My mom? Ah, no. If my mom loves you, she delegates work to you." Which is true, I delegate work only to those I highly respect and trust—those I love!

My single niece lived with us for a year, and we all did our love language test when she moved in. Bill, my son Caleb, and my niece all ranked "quality time" as their top love language. I was frightened to death! I could never meet all their needs for quality time. So I said, "Look at these results. I am opting out of this expectation. I promise that I will give each of you all the time I can, but you all need to commit to meet each other's needs on this one." They did, and the household worked better than it would have otherwise.

Knowing motivation, love language, and conflict-resolution styles can also help if you have roommates. Life is easier and unity can be maintained if you know the inner wirings of those you live with. So how do you prefer to be loved?

Personal Love Language Profile [5]

> My love language is (check one):
>
> ☐ *Words of affirmation*
>
> ☐ *Physical touch*
>
> ☐ *Quality time*
>
> ☐ *Acts of service*
>
> ☐ *Gifts*

Birth Order

Your placement in the family you grew up in affected who you are today. Dr. Kevin Leman, in *The New Birth Order Book*, offers a short sample quiz to help the reader get a quick grasp of birth order:

Which of the following sets of birth-order traits fits you best?

A. Perfectionist, reliable, conscientious, list maker, well organized, hard-driving, natural leader, critical, serious, scholarly, logical, doesn't like surprises, loves computers.

B. Mediator, compromising, diplomatic, avoids conflict, independent, loyal to peers, many friends, a maverick, secretive, unspoiled.

C. Manipulative, charming, blames others, attention seeker, tenacious, people person, natural salesperson, precocious, engaging, affectionate, loves surprises.

D. Little adult by age seven, very thorough, deliberate, high achiever, self-motivated, fearful, cautious, voracious reader, black-and-white thinker, uses "very," "extremely," and "exactly" a lot, can't bear to fail, has very high expectations for self, more comfortable with people who are older or younger. [6]

If you noted that the test seemed rather easy because A, B, C listed traits of the oldest right on down to the youngest in the family, you are right. If you picked list A, it's a very good bet you are the firstborn in your family. If you chose list B, chances are you are a middle child. If list C seemed to relate best to who you are, it's likely you are the baby in the family. But what about list D? It describes the only child.

It is interesting to note that two middle children have the best odds at long-term love because they are trained to negotiate and compromise as part of the family dynamic. Two firstborns need lots of relational training because they will both want to be in charge. An only child is typically harder on himself than anyone else. Babies of the family tend to like to be the center of attention.

The upside of firstborns is their natural leadership skills.

The upside of middle kids is their people and mediator skills.

The upside of babies is their natural persuasive and sales skills.

The upside of only children is their diligence and attention to excellence.

Personal Birth-Order Profile[7]

My birth order is _____.

My best trait because of my role in my family of origin is _____.

Relax and Recharge Style

How we get the most from our downtime is an essential item to know—just ask anyone who has gone on vacation with a group of friends. To some, relaxing is a week filled with strenuous days of hiking, swimming, golf, tennis, cycling, and kayaking. Others picture vacation workouts as torture. The hardest workout they want is to get up, change out of pj's into a swimsuit, and lie in a hammock and read or nap the day away. Some want to tour and cram in as many "things one must see" as they can. Still others picture a real vacation as long, meaningful walks and talks. Their friend might be just as happy to shop alone and take home a suitcase of great buys.

Know what helps you relax and know who else might relax in your same style before you create a vacation plan together. You can combine a variety of people and relaxation styles on a vacation *if* you discuss ahead of time one simple question, "What one thing do you want to see happen on vacation that will help you come home relaxed and refreshed?" Then decide to offer some group time and a lot of solo or smaller group time so that everyone's needs get met.

So what is your relax and recharge style?

Busy bee: Even on vacation busy bees have a to-do list. They come into a vacation or day off with a schedule and plan.

Social butterfly: These people believe vacations are all about relationships, so driving two days each way on a five-day trip is just fine if they get to see their relatives.

Waiting walking stick: Walking sticks are bugs that sit all day. In the same way, these people like to sit still on vacation or a day off. Give them a hammock and a book and they're happy.

Active ant: These people enjoy activities and athletics on their days off. You'll find them jet skiing, kayaking, snowboarding, hiking, and the like.

Luggage ladybug: Ladybugs prefer guided tours, group outings, and professionals in charge of their free time.

If you talk through your downtime style in advance, less of your free time will be used for arguments and more of it used for fun activities!

Personal Relax-and-Recharge Profile[8]

My recharging style is _____.

My perfect vacation would be _____.

Your Unique Gift

We each have at least one spiritual gift. The moment you began a relationship with Jesus, God entrusted you with a gift so that His name would be glorified through your life. Sort through the list below. This is not an exhaustive list of gifts but rather a place to begin to explore what your gift might be as you serve others.

Administration: directing projects (Romans 12:8; 1 Corinthians 12:5,28).

Craftsmanship and artistry: using your hands to create or build so that others are pointed toward God (Exodus 30:22-25; 2 Chronicles 34:9-13; Acts 16:14; 18:3).

Evangelism: communicating spiritual truth to lead someone to a personal relationship with God (Acts 5:42; Romans 10:15; Ephesians 4:11; 2 Timothy 4:5).

Exhortation: encouraging people and walking alongside them to bring out the best in them (Romans 12:8; 1 Corinthians 2:1-2; 2 Corinthians 9:2).

Giving: being a faithful steward of the resources God has entrusted to you and sharing with others (Mark 12:41-44; Luke 18:12; Romans 12:8; 2 Corinthians 8:1-7).

Helps and serving: caring for others by working behind the scenes (Mark 2:3-4; Luke 22:22-27; Romans 12:7; 16:1-2; 1 Corinthians 12:28; 1 Timothy 6:2; 1 Peter 4:9-10).

Hospitality: using the home or other resources to make people feel included and welcomed (Acts 16:15; 21:16-17; Romans 12:9-13; 16:23).

Intercession: devoting extended time and energy to pray for others (Acts 12:1-17; 16:25-31; Colossians 4:12; 1 Timothy 2:1-8).

Knowledge: sharing truth that helps people live in a productive, healthy manner (Romans 15:14; 1 Corinthians 12:8; 13:8).

Leadership: setting an example for other people to follow (1 Timothy 5:17).

Mercy: showing compassion and meeting needs (Luke 10:33-35; Acts 9:36; 16:33-34; Romans 12:8).

Music: singing or playing instruments to turn hearts toward God (1 Samuel 16:16; 1 Chronicles 16:41-42; 2 Chronicles 5:12-13).

Prophecy: publicly proclaiming truth (1 Corinthians 12:10; 13:2; 14:1).

Teaching: explaining spiritual truth to others and helping them apply it (Romans 12:7; 1 Corinthians 12:28; Ephesians 4:11; 1 Timothy 3:2).

Wisdom: applying knowledge with discretion and insight (2 Chronicles 1:11-12; Proverbs 1:2; 2:10).

Writing: communicating information to help others grow in faith, develop life skills, or turn toward God (Psalm 45:1; Philippians 3:1; 1 Timothy 3:14-15).

The best way to discern your gifts is to pick out four or five you think might be your gifts and then try them out. If people are affected positively by your efforts, that is confirmation. If you enjoy life more when using that gift, that is confirmation. If you see tangible, long-lasting fruit from using the gift, that is confirmation.

When you're dating, this is a vital area to discuss, especially if the person you are dating is someone you may want to marry. For example, if you believe you are called into full-time vocational ministry in order to fully use your gifts, your potential mate needs to be called too or life in ministry will be a constant source of frustration and disagreement. Ministry isn't a job; it's a lifestyle. You can have any of the gifts and feel called to ministry. It isn't the gift that matters. Many gifts can mesh to make a strong ministry team and ministry family. But if you are called to ministry, permanently connect your life only to someone who feels called to ministry as well.[9]

I believe my top three gifts might be:

1.

2.

3.

Financial Style

In *A Woman's Guide to Family Finances*, Ellie Kay describes several money-management styles. We've adapted these for both genders and condensed their descriptions. So what is your money style?

Power Paul (or Polly): The person with the money has the power.

Secure Samantha (or Sam): This person is a born saver who feels secure only if she saves "just a little more." Fear is an underlying emotion.

Tightwad Tilly (or Tom): Beyond frugal, this person often holds on to money instead of using it for positive purposes.

Worrywart Ward (or Wanda): This person obsesses about money. He is held captive by "what ifs." *What if people love me only for my money? What if I make a bad investment?* He thinks about money too much.

Spendthrift Steve (or Stephanie): If this person has a dollar, he needs to spend it.

Feel good Francine (or Frank): If this person feels bad, off she goes to the mall.

Love ya Louie (or Louise): This person uses money to try to make people feel good about him.

Balanced Betty (or Bob): This person has good financial habits, and her attitudes toward money are balanced and healthy.

We all want to think of ourselves as a balanced Betty or Bob, but which of the others describes your #2 money motivator?

Personal Financial Profile

My preferred money style is _____.

My #2 style is _____.

One step I can take to be more balanced with money
is _____.[10]

Parenting Style

Some of you are single parents. You have a parenting style that guides your actions and decisions with your children. The way you parent is a combination of what you saw modeled by your parents and what you have learned on your own. Good parenting is not automatic. Becoming a good parent is a process, and anyone can learn to become a better parent than he or she is currently. The most effective parenting is proactive and it requires a lot of energy and focus to achieve. You can begin to be a proactive parent by identifying your starting point and creating a plan for growth.

Which of these styles best describes you as a parent?

> *Permissive*: These parents border on apathy or neglect. They are too busy, too broken, or too self-absorbed to care.

> *Popular*: These parents are so concerned about being a friend to their child that they won't risk the friendship by providing rules, boundaries, or discipline.

> *Paranoid*: These parents worry about everything and make decisions based upon fear.

> *Prescriptive*: These parents wait until issues become problems before they act.

> *Power-hungry*: These parents are harsh and often react and discipline in out-of-control anger if their children make them look bad in front of others.

> *Proactive*: These parents prayerfully set goals, make plans, and discuss parenting choices ahead of time to guide and lead a child forward.

If your parenting style is anything except proactive, we encourage you to take some parenting courses. Otherwise, your parenting style may drive away friends and potential marriage partners. Out-of-control kids make people want to stay away from you and your family. If you are a paranoid or power-hungry parent, others will feel uncomfortable for your children when they are around you.

Personal Parenting Profile

> My parenting style tends to be _____, but I want to be proactive by improving in my _____.[11]

The Power of Acceptance

Now that you're aware of these various styles of learning and motivation, what do you do with the information? You have some choices. You can use what you've learned as an advantage to manipulate others. Or you can use it to excuse your own unhealthy behaviors. Of course neither of these options is a wise choice because God wants you to grow in grace and to mature in your areas of weakness.

A much more useful approach is to explore your strengths and uniqueness so you can use these to help others. At the same time, look for the strengths and uniqueness in others so you can motivate them to further God's plan of love around the world. It doesn't take much to realize that peace in relationships will be the result. This type of active acceptance draws the praise of God into our lives like a magnet, causing our influence to be more than natural (Romans 15:7).

Just for Fun

One day an employee sent a letter to his boss asking for a raise.

Dear Bo$$

In thi$ life, we all need $ome thing mo$t de$perately. I think you $hould be under$tanding of the need$ of u$ worker$ who have given $o much $upport including $weat and $ervice to your company.

I am $ure you will gue$$ what I mean and re$pond $oon.

Your$ $incerely,
Norman $oh

The next day, the employee received this letter of reply:

Dear NOrman,

I kNOw you have been working very hard. NOwadays, NOthing much has changed. You must have NOticed that our company is NOt doing NOticeably well as yet.

NOw the newspapers are saying the world's leading ecoNO-mists are NOt sure if the United States may go into aNOther recession. After the NOvember presidential elections things may turn bad.

I have NOthing more to add NOw. You kNOw what I mean.

Yours truly,
Manager[12]

CHAPTER 5

Decide to Wait

"The fruit of the Spirit is…patience."

Galatians 5:22

We know, we know. You don't want to hear it. You think this chapter is about patiently waiting until God brings the right person into your life. You've heard it all before. Be content. Be happy with yourself. Don't get too involved until the right one comes along. Our favorite new bit of advice on this waiting game is, "Marriage is like flies on a screen door. Those on the outside want in, and those on the inside want out."

Well, this chapter is not really about relationships. We don't think it matters whether you get married or not. Being single is just as good as being married. In fact, the Bible says single people have an advantage, if they can accept it. Here's some evidence God actually believes this. The apostle Paul, a single man, wrote:

> It is good for a man not to marry…I wish that all men were as I am. But each man has his own gift from God…Now to the unmarried and the widows I say: It is good for them to stay unmarried, as I am.

Did you catch this? Singleness is a gift. Why is it a gift?

> I would like you to be free from concern. An unmarried man is concerned about the Lord's affairs—how he can please the Lord. But a married man is concerned about the affairs of

this world—how he can please his wife—and his interests are divided. An unmarried woman or virgin is concerned about the Lord's affairs: Her aim is to be devoted to the Lord in both body and spirit. But a married woman is concerned about the affairs of this world—how she can please her husband. I am saying this for your own good, not to restrict you, but that you may live in a right way in undivided devotion to the Lord (1 Corinthians 7:1, 7-8, 32-35).

Singleness is a gift because it saves you a whole lot of headaches and frees you to be devoted to Jesus.

Guys, here is just one example of some of the headache you are saved from as a single. Someone told us recently, "Remember back in junior high when all the girls were taken out of class for a special program on what happens to their body when they mature? The girls were told they would go through a menstrual cycle once a month for much of their adult lives. Of course, the girls' frantic response was, 'Will this bleeding hurt?' And the answer was, 'It won't hurt you, but it will hurt everyone around you!'"

Ladies, you are also saved from trouble if you are single. Consider some of these convictions of men:

- "Because I'm a man, when I lock my keys in the car, I will fiddle with a coat hanger long after hypothermia has set in. Calling AAA is not an option. I will win."

- "Because I'm a man, I can be relied upon to purchase basic groceries at the store, like milk or bread. I cannot be expected to find exotic items like cumin or tofu. For all I know, these are the same thing."

- "Because I'm a man, when one of our appliances stops working, I will insist on taking it apart, despite evidence that this will cost me twice as much once the repairman gets here and has to put it back together."

- "Because I'm a man, I think what you're wearing is fine. I thought what you were wearing five minutes ago was fine too. Either pair of shoes is fine. With the belt or without it looks fine. Your hair is fine. You look fine. Can we just go now?"

And girls you do look fine, but now you know that you won't have to stand in the cold wondering why you can't just call AAA for a tow, your appliances are in one piece, and you own the remote!

So all of life isn't about waiting for the right one, but most of life is about waiting for God's best in all areas. What really does matter is the quality of your life, and a big part of the formula is learning how to wait.

The Waiting Room

Even a cursory reading of the Bible demonstrates that learning to wait is one of life's primary goals.

> In the morning, O LORD, you hear my voice;
>> in the morning I lay my requests before you
>> and wait in expectation.
>>> (Psalm 5:3)
>
> Wait for the LORD;
>> be strong and take heart
>> and wait for the LORD.
>>> (Psalm 27:14)
>
> I wait for the LORD, my soul waits,
>> and in his word I put my hope.
>>> (Psalm 130:5)
>
> Yet the LORD longs to be gracious to you;
>> he rises to show you compassion.
> For the LORD is a God of justice.
>> Blessed are all who wait for him!
>>> (Isaiah 30:18)
>
> It is good to wait quietly
>> for the salvation of the LORD.
>>> (Lamentations 3:26)

Waiting has always been hard for people. Abraham and Sarah grew tired of waiting for God to give them the heir He had promised, so Abraham impregnated Sarah's servant, Hagar, and Ishmael was born. The two nations that were spawned from Isaac, the child of promise, and Ishmael have been at odds with one another ever since.

In 1 Samuel 28, King Saul had a problem. Samuel, his primary advisor and connection to God, had died, and the Philistines were preparing to do battle with Israel. Normally, Saul would have asked Samuel for God's marching orders, but Samuel was no longer around. Saul inquired directly of the Lord, but "the LORD did not answer him" (v. 6). The appropriate response would have been to wait for the Lord. Jewish history is filled with accounts of miraculous victories as Israel's leaders waited for God's instructions and His deliverance. But waiting is hard, and Saul lost patience. In fear, he consulted a medium, which led to a frightful encounter with Samuel and a devastating defeat in battle.

In Matthew 20, we get a glimpse into the heart of the mother of James and John, two of the twelve apostles. She loved her sons and was proud that they were following Jesus, and she obviously recognized the authority of their master when she came to Him with this request: "Grant that one of these two sons of mine may sit at your right and the other at your left in your kingdom" (v. 21). Her desire was a good one; the problem was in her timing.

The earthly ministry of Jesus was a time of humble service as He made His way to the cross. The boys are not innocent in this because they boldly proclaimed they could endure whatever hardship might be involved even though they didn't fully understand the suffering to come. The appropriate response would have been to ask Jesus to explain His kingdom plan rather than impose their idea of the plan. They just got in a hurry and caused tension among the other apostles. In His masterful way, Jesus pulled the men together and pointed out one of His most important principles: "Whoever wants to become great among you must be your servant" (v. 26).

Things are not any easier today. We live in a society that does not like to wait. Technology has made almost every area of life more efficient. Fast-food restaurants continue to multiply despite numerous health warnings. Smartphones are commonplace with their ability to deliver email and text messages and to connect to social networking sites. We want to connect now. We want to know now. We want to acquire now. We want leaders who can make decisions and solve complex problems now. In a word, we are about *now*, and it's hard to wait in a society that is all about now. As a result, most of us are discontent even though we have more advantages than any generation before us.

Those who learn to wait, however, find that the journey of life maintains its fascination. In learning to wait, we can avoid the pitfalls of the pressure to rush in, rush on, or rush through.

Meet Josh

If you were to meet Josh today, you would conclude that he is a successful, smart, handsome, articulate, and very normal person. He currently serves as a lawyer in the Judge Advocate General's (JAG) Corps. To maintain his position, he has to pass the Army Physical Fitness Test (APFT) with a minimum score of 180. He recently aced the test by scoring a 291 out of 300 and earned the Army Physical Fitness Badge. He sits up straight, engages in intelligent conversation, and exudes confidence. He is a young man with many of the qualities we all want in our lives. The only thing that would clue you into his journey is the way he does sit-ups since he can't bend his back. He has overcome remarkable odds, and he would be the first to tell you that he has become who he is by learning to wait.

Josh was born missing a rib and half the connecting vertebra. To compensate for those missing parts, his spine curved, and he was diagnosed with congenital scoliosis at age three. Prior to puberty, his back developed a curvature of 14 degrees, which was monitored annually. Visits to the orthopedist and multiple X-rays became a normal occurrence, and it never occurred to him that his life was any different than his peers. "Unless I stood and attempted to touch my toes," Josh says, "the curvature of my spine was not outwardly visible, and I was never forced to wear one of those garish and unseemly braces."

Around the age of 15, as rapid physical growth proved too much for his spine, his curvature increased to a frightening 56 degrees. He was referred to a specialist in another city while the frequency of visits to the doctor's office increased. There were, however, no outward signs betraying his condition to his peers, so he navigated his sophomore year in high school rather well. Since he felt no side effects, he concluded he could do what he wanted and made plans to try out for the track team. He was especially interested in pole vaulting.

Shortly before track season began, a surgeon informed him that an operation to correct his spine was a necessary and immediate need. Josh preferred to wait until summer, but his doctor told him he would be a hunchback by the time he was 21 if he didn't have the surgery right away. It was agonizing for a 15-year-old to be forced to wait on track competition with the possibility that it might never happen.

It Is Good to Wait

We've lost sight of the fact that some of the best things in life come to us through waiting. Those who have disciplined themselves to wait discover skills, opportunities, and influence that their peers tend to miss.

Waiting Makes Us Less Defensive

Psalm 33:20 states, "We wait in hope for the LORD; he is our help and our shield." Being defensive is one of the most common reactions in relationships. We are all afraid of being criticized, scrutinized, and analyzed. Something is said early in a conversation that makes us wary, and we respond by pulling back and protecting ourselves. Jesus said He would be our shield and protect us, but we have a hard time believing He will step in. So we take matters into our own hands and push people away with our words.

We recently watched the following interaction between two friends. Let's call them Beth and Gena:

"How do you feel when I get really stressed and kind of freak out?" Beth asked.

"I guess I'm okay with it," Gena said. "But I am not responsible for your feelings, so don't put that on me."

We agree that friends are not responsible for each other's feelings, but that wasn't Beth's question. She was trying to open a significant conversation where they could share honestly, but Gena grew instantly defensive. She felt imposed upon and manipulated without reason.

This kind of thing happens because we feel vulnerable. Waiting helps us realize that God has our back and will shield us from trouble so we don't have to guard ourselves as carefully. We aren't suggesting that you foolishly ignore common-sense steps to stay safe. We are simply saying that you don't have to live self-consciously afraid that others will take advantage of you when you learn to wait on the Lord.

Waiting Helps Us Stay Focused on Our Career Goals

When you seek to have a career that brings you satisfaction and the potential for success, you enter a competitive world. You will notice along the way that many people are willing to do whatever it takes to succeed. They manipulate, shade the truth, take credit for what they didn't do, blame others for what they did do, and use others to reach selfish goals. This tactic is often successful in the short run. Some of the richest and most powerful people have operated this way, but it is always short-lived.

At some time, in some way, bad decisions catch up with people. Broken relationships, lost opportunities, or lonely existences eventually characterize people who use others. In the short term, however, it can appear that living with integrity and convictions leads to second place. The only way to avoid this illusion is to be willing to wait.

> Be still before the LORD and wait patiently for him;
>   do not fret when men succeed in their ways,
>   when they carry out their wicked schemes.
>   (Psalm 37:7)

> Wait for the LORD
>   and keep his way.
> He will exalt you to inherit the land;
>   when the wicked are cut off, you will see it.
>   (Psalm 37:34)

Waiting Helps Us Resist Taking Revenge

Your life, like our lives, is littered with tough circumstances. You have suffered disappointments and setbacks. People have taken advantage of you, lied to you, or frustrated your plans. The natural inclination is to take revenge—to look for a way to set things straight. If you do not have the courage to confront, you will settle into sadness or self-pity. Learning to wait helps you refocus with the confidence that Jesus will make everything right. No one gets away with anything because all of us will give an account one day.

Therefore judge nothing before the appointed time; wait till the Lord comes. He will bring to light what is hidden in darkness and will expose the motives of men's hearts. At that time each will receive his praise from God (1 Corinthians 4:5).

Do not say, "I'll pay you back for this wrong!"
Wait for the LORD, and he will deliver you.
(Proverbs 20:22)

When you are willing to wait for God to settle accounts, you replace revenge with forgiveness. If you honestly believe that Jesus will one day make all things right, you will be willing to make Colossians 3:13 a theme of your life: "Bear with each other and forgive whatever grievances you may have against one another. Forgive as the Lord forgave you."

We have concluded that forgiveness is the defining issue of life. Those who find the courage to forgive live with clean hearts, clear focus, and a committed purpose. Those who refuse to forgive get infected with bitterness, which leads to anger, inactivity, depression, underachieving, and a number of other negative symptoms that sap your soul of energy. It would be easy for us to be bitter toward an alcoholic father with a severe rage issue and a controlling mother who was afraid of everyone and everything. We, however, decided that we did not want the unhealthy people in our lives to be a controlling influence.

If you are willing to wait, you will decide to forgive also.

So what exactly is forgiveness and how do you live it out in your life?

First, let's talk about what forgiveness is not. Forgiveness is not "just letting it go." It's easy to think that forgiveness is an attempt to dismiss the hurt from our souls. We think that we should be able to just let go of the disappointments, pain, and betrayals of life. This is a vain attempt to put our mind and heart in neutral rather than applying true forgiveness.

Forgiveness is not saying, "It's okay." Many of us have a habit of saying to someone who apologizes, "It's okay." These words are a sincere attempt to move forward rather than dwell on the past, but they fall short of accomplishing forgiveness. Saying, "It's okay," is appropriate when you have a difference of opinion with another person, but forgiveness is necessary when something wrong was done.

Forgiveness is not denial. When your heart is hurting, it's easy to shove things under the rug in an attempt to feel better. As you continue to push things under the rug, the path of your life gets very bumpy, and you begin to trip over the thoughts and emotions you were trying to avoid.

Forgiveness is not forgetting. When you choose to forgive, you do not lose your memory. Just the opposite usually happens when you forgive rather than feel sorry for yourself. You will remember what happened in vivid detail, but the story begins to change. When Jesus gets involved with the story of your life, it becomes more than a tale of hurt and pain. It becomes a story of redemption, which means God takes the broken parts of your life and fashions them into something that will amaze you. There is no formula for what God creates out of the ashes, but He is a master at forming influential lives out of frustrating disappointments.

Finally, forgiveness is not reconciliation. Forgiveness is a decision you make to not allow anyone but God to control your emotional and spiritual life. It is a vertical activity between you and God that involves nobody else. The goal of forgiveness is to defeat bitterness as part of your strategy to "guard your heart, for it is the wellspring of life" (Proverbs 4:23). It is your commitment to keep your spiritual, emotional, and social being vital, strong and vibrant.

Reconciliation, on the other hand, is a decision to restore a broken or hurting relationship, and this requires two people to actively participate. Both individuals must forgive any wrong against them, and they must repent from anything they have done to hurt the relationship. Without both ingredients, the relationship cannot truly be reconciled.

As a result, it is possible to forgive everyone for everything, but it may not be possible to reconcile with everyone. Those who will not repent are likely to repeat the behavior that created the hurt in the first place. In these instances, forgiveness should be followed by setting boundaries that restrict or block the relationship so that the unhealthy actions of the other person no longer influence your life.

The operative question then is, "How do you forgive another person?" This became a very important question for us, so we went looking for the answer. We explored what it would look like if we applied the gospel of Christ, the greatest example of forgiveness on earth, to our relationships. What we came up with is the following six statements of forgiveness:

1. I forgive _____ for _____.
   (name the person)   (name the offense)

2. I affirm that what happened was wrong.

3. I do not expect this person to make up for what he or she has done.

4. I will not use what happened to define who this person is.

5. I will not attempt to manipulate this person with this offense.

6. I will not allow what happened to stop my personal growth.

These statements form a working definition for forgiveness. When you become aware of something that you need to forgive someone for, say these statements out loud, inserting the name of the person and the specific offense. If you can sincerely say all six statements, you have forgiven that person. If you cannot get through them all, you aren't quite ready. So stop, ask God to get you ready, and try again tomorrow.

I (Bill) am in the habit of praying the following every day: "Jesus, please bring to my mind anything I need to forgive that you know I am ready to forgive today." If anything comes to mind, I say the six statements over this situation. If nothing comes to mind, I thank Jesus for the day off and don't worry about it. This puts Jesus rather than my self-effort in charge of the process. This has proven to be quite helpful.

We all have a habit of deceiving ourselves when it comes to matters of the heart. And forgiveness is definitely a matter of the heart. Since the heart cannot be trusted to navigate the painful path on its own, Jeremiah revealed the secret for us:

> The heart is deceitful above all things
>   and beyond cure.
>   Who can understand it?
> "I the LORD search the heart
>   and examine the mind,
> to reward a man according to his conduct,
>   according to what his deeds deserve."
>   (Jeremiah 17:9-10)

When you give Jesus the opportunity each day to search your heart, the path may not be easier, but it is certainly a lot clearer.

Waiting Helps Us Feel Young

You have lived long enough to know that life constantly takes. You are expected to give of your time, your money, your wisdom, your friendship, your skills, and your focus. In the process, you get drained, especially when you have to do things that are unattractive to you. It's a compliment to you that others want what you can give, but it also depletes your energy. To keep functioning well, you need a way to recharge and refresh. The prophet Isaiah reminds us that waiting is one way of restoring our enthusiasm:

> He gives power to the faint,
>> and to him who has no might he increases strength.
> Even youths shall faint and be weary,
>> and young men shall fall exhausted;
> but they who wait for the LORD shall renew their strength;
>> they shall mount up with wings like eagles;
> they shall run and not be weary;
>> they shall walk and not faint.
>> (Isaiah 40:29-31 ESV)

In addition, waiting does a number of things to keep our hearts soft and responsive:

Waiting Builds Hope

> But the eyes of the LORD are on those who fear him,
>> on those whose hope is in his unfailing love...
> We wait in hope for the LORD;
>> he is our help and our shield.
> In him our hearts rejoice,
>> for we trust in his holy name.
>> (Psalm 33:18,20-21)

Waiting Trains Us to Listen to God

> I wait for you, O LORD;
>> you will answer, O Lord my God.
>> (Psalm 38:15)

Waiting Makes Us More Stable

> I waited patiently for the LORD;
>> he turned to me and heard my cry.
> He lifted me out of the slimy pit,
>> out of the mud and mire;
> he set my feet on a rock
>> and gave me a firm place to stand.
>>> (Psalm 40:1-2)

Waiting Helps Us Experience God's Compassion

> Yet the LORD longs to be gracious to you;
>> he rises to show you compassion.
> For the LORD is a God of justice.
>> Blessed are all who wait for him!
>>> (Isaiah 30:18)

Josh's Active Waiting Period

Once Josh's surgery was scheduled, waiting became a whirlwind of activity. An MRI was necessary to determine whether the spinal cord was improperly wrapped around Josh's bizarrely curved spine. The doctors were concerned about the increased possibility of damage and paralysis during surgery. Also, blood needed to be stockpiled. Josh and his father both have O-positive blood, so they donated ahead of time just in case complications arose.

On April 3, 1999, a new season of waiting began. Josh's classmates were enjoying the freedom and merriment of spring break while he "vacationed" in the hospital. Despite his inner protests, Josh got his initiation into the fact that waiting forces us to choose whether we will live by fear or by faith. He transparently admits, "I realized that if I came out of that surgery paralyzed, I would not want to live. I was an active soccer player and had planned on running track that spring, until the surgery was scheduled. In hindsight, I realize that life would not have ended had I become a paraplegic, but as a 16-year-old, that was my one true concern."

Waiting also taught Josh that God looks for ways, sometimes large, sometimes small, to encourage us in the midst of the journey. Entering

Spectrum Health Hospital in Grand Rapids, Michigan, was intimidating. Exchanging his clothes for a hospital gown was embarrassing. Receiving general anesthesia caused him to feel out of control. But amidst these challenges, the medical resident who assisted in the surgery had attended medical school at the University of Michigan, Josh's favorite school.

Waiting Is Active

A lot of people find waiting unattractive because they think it's a passive experience. We wait around doing nothing while we wait for God to do something. The good news is that waiting is an active pursuit. Psalm 37 describes the active nature of waiting by outlining the activities that characterize the life of one who knows how to wait.

> Trust in the LORD and do good;
>> dwell in the land and enjoy safe pasture.
> Delight yourself in the LORD
>> and he will give you the desires of your heart.
> Commit your way to the LORD;
>> trust in him and he will do this:
> He will make your righteousness shine like the dawn,
>> the justice of your cause like the noonday sun.
> Be still before the LORD
>> and wait patiently for him;
> do not fret when men succeed in their ways,
>> when they carry out their wicked schemes.
> Refrain from anger and turn from wrath;
>> do not fret—it leads only to evil.
>> (vv. 3-8)

What to Do While Waiting

Take care of current responsibilities (v. 3). God made people to work and be responsible. When God created Adam and Eve, He quickly gave them a job to do. They were to rule over the other creatures God had made and to be the caretakers of the Garden of Eden (Genesis 1:27-28; 2:15).

People are designed by God to be productive. When you're busy with a job, a hobby, a ministry, or a project, you think clearer, relate to others better, and have a healthier sense of well-being. You want to keep yourself alert and ready for action. Therefore, waiting begins with a fervent commitment to pursue your God-given responsibilities.

Pursue an affectionate relationship with God (v. 4). Waiting is all about being in partnership with God. He has a plan for your life, and He is preparing you to fit into that plan in the right way at the right time. Since the plan revolves around Him, part of waiting is using your time to develop an active relationship with your Savior.

Set goals, make a plan, and commit it to the Lord (v. 5). Since you are a full partner in this venture, you have the freedom and a mandate to make plans. God encourages you to think ahead, dream of what you want to accomplish, and set a plan for getting there. Our plans involve waiting because there is so much we cannot control. We can make plans, but we can't cause the weather to cooperate. We can set goals, but we can't force the economy to provide the resources to make them all happen. We can commit our plans to the Lord, but we cannot guarantee that He will say yes. Although we can't assure that our goals and plans will be accomplished, they keep us sharp. They keep us thinking and adaptable so when the opportunity breaks open, we are ready to move.

Pursue your purpose and fight against the tendency to compare your life to others (v. 7). You are a unique person with a unique place in God's plan. This is so easy to say that you would think everyone agrees and readily accepts that it's true. Most of us, however, bounce back and forth between two unsupportable positions.

The first is pride. We just think too much of ourselves. We act as though we created our lives and we can do whatever we want, whenever we want, however we want. The other is the notion that we are worthless or meaningless or that we don't count as much as others. We act as if God created filler people to take up space while the important people participate in real life.

We are neither ordinary nor extraordinary. We are unique. When you compare yourself with others, you will always conclude that you are either better or worse than they are. When you compare yourself against your potential, you have the opportunity to realize that only you can accomplish what you were designed for. Whether it's a big contribution or a small one, it is your contribution. When waiting includes discovering your unique contribution to life, the waiting period becomes one of the most valuable times of your life.

We often hear complaints from those in God's waiting room.

"Why isn't God bringing me a job?" (Have you created the résumé, made calls, used social media and your friendship circle to let folks know you are looking? Have you gone to job fairs, career counselors, headhunters, or your college placement program?)

"Why am I still waiting for a new place to live?" (Have you placed calls to rental agencies, property management companies, real estate agents? Have you communicated with friends and family that you are looking and what you are praying God provides?)

"When will God bring me Mr. Right, Mrs. Amazing?" (Have you been out meeting new people, going to new places, creating new connections through social media or other trustworthy sources? Have you hosted or planned singles conferences, dinner parties, special events? Are you networking where quality singles would be found: volunteering, leading ministries, serving in missions, ministering to the military or those in seminary?)

Waiting is not sedentary. That degree will not come if you never apply to graduate school. That business opportunity will not come if you are home playing Xbox. That future partner will likely not arrive in your life if you do the same thing with the same people day after day. Waiting is active, so ask God what He wants you to do while you wait.

While writing this book, Bill and I hosted a few singles for dinner parties and focus groups. Many of the singles didn't know anyone at these dinners other than us, but they came anyway. Those who did made new friends; some even went on dates. They expanded their friendship circle with their willingness to say yes to a healthy opportunity.

Being willing to risk, to keep taking action, to keep busy doing good things keeps you in a place where God can steer you. Bill likes to call this, "Keeping your boat in the water." When your boat is in the water and your oar is in hand, you can go for the ride of your life as God directs the tides and currents.

Two singles at one of the events were Mark and Marissa. Both were quality singles in their mid-twenties with well-established careers—so well-established they had a hard time meeting new people. We know this is a struggle for many adults because our lives become much more compartmentalized as we get older. Rather than spending all day at school with hundreds of other students, we commit to work with a relatively small group of people.

Mark and Marissa each had a desire to someday marry, but until they met the right person they kept themselves busy. Marissa traveled, gardened, taught school and had an active social life with friends and with her Bible study group. She was busy living all out for God.

Mark served in missions, made cross-country and West Coast bike trips, helped launch a couple ministries by volunteering his computer skills and landed a prosperous accounting job. He led a community group of singles at his church, and a smaller Bible study guys group. He was busy living all out for God.

Someone mentioned to Mark that he might want to check into some of the online connection sites because he was so busy. He had little social time and he felt like he had met most everyone in his church who was datable. He decided to check them out.

Characteristics of an Online Meeting Site You Can Trust

- The focus is on your character before your looks
- There are a significant number of questions about your purpose in life
- Compatibility is measured based on convictions and commitments rather than social preferences
- Your privacy is protected until you are ready to remove it
- Spiritual preferences and maturity is rated and displayed
- Tips are given for building a friendship, not just finding dates (one of the highest predictors of marital success is the friendship of the partners)

Marissa's dad had been friends with the creator of one of these sites so he suggested to her that, since she was so busy in her career, she might try it out. You see where the story is going don't you? They met online even though they lived in the same city. They were attracted to each other because they were looking for someone busy serving God. They dated and were in premarital counseling with Bill during the time we wrote this book. On the day before we turned in the manuscript, Bill performed their wedding ceremony.

We rejoice with them even though we know it doesn't work out like this for everyone. Online sites are just one way of networking with other individuals. They work for some people and don't work for others. The key is to find healthy ways to keep increasing your network of friends so you continue to grow and your opportunities continue to expand.

Why Wait?

Waiting helps us live with the why questions of life. It isn't hard to find circumstances that cause us to question why. Hard things happen and unexpected circumstances hinder our progress. We believe this is why James 1:2-5 gets so many people's attention: "Consider it pure joy…whenever you face trials of many kinds…If any of you lacks wisdom, he should ask God…and it will be given to him."

When setbacks happen, it's natural to ask why. When you've given your best efforts and things didn't work out, it's natural to ask why. When someone less deserving than you gets promoted or prospers, it's natural to ask why. But this question seldom gets answered. If anyone deserved an answer it was Job, and he was never told why he had to suffer. The reality is that we can figure out what to do in our lives even when we don't know why things have turned out the way they have. Waiting helps us learn to ask for wisdom when we want to ask why.

Josh had to wrestle with the intense waiting that causes us all to ask why without ever getting satisfactory answers. In layman's terms, Josh underwent "full spinal fusion," an operation that lasted approximately six hours. Multiple vertebrae were fused together, sandwiched between two titanium rods. Periodically throughout the surgery, Josh was roused from medically induced sleep and asked to move or wiggle his toes and feet. The doctors wanted to confirm that his spinal cord had not been traumatized as they straightened his spine. The goal, of course, was to arrest the increasing curvature of the spine and to make permanent a livable, though imperfect, curve. The challenge for the surgeon was determining just how much correction he could accomplish without damaging the spinal cord and inducing paralysis.

"Going into the surgery," Josh reflects, "my surgeon informed me that full spinal fusion is the most painful surgery someone my age could experience." Josh braced himself for the agony that would follow, but no one anticipated that the tube that would feed painkilling medicine directly to his back would come unattached and be unnoticed for almost 16 hours.

"I've always lived an active lifestyle, and I've had a litany of broken bones as well as a few concussions. These all caused varying degrees of physical agony, but the immediate aftermath of that surgery was the worst pain I have ever experienced. I wouldn't even want people I don't like to be in that much suffering. And it wouldn't stop. Throughout those 16 hours, I lay on my back moaning and groaning. My prone position hid from the nurses the plight of my disconnected tube. I was exhausted and in continual pain. I begged the nurses and my mother to give me more medicine, but they didn't want to give me too much morphine through the catheter in my arm, so their ability to assuage my pain was negligible. We all remained unaware that the real answer to my pain lay underneath me."

During those 16 hours, Josh wondered why. "I was a bit bewildered as to why I was experiencing such dramatic pain when I knew so many people had me in their prayers. I repeatedly asked my mother, 'Are you praying for me? Is Grandma praying for me? Are people praying for me?'"

They were all praying, but the pain persisted. Even looking back on the event, the answers are elusive. Why did God allow the tube to disconnect? How come no one noticed, which caused Josh to suffer for hours without relief?

Often waiting for answers is all we get.

Josh learned that waiting leads us to choose whether we will respond positively or negatively to life's challenges. All of us will experience tough times because we live in an imperfect world. We have no choice over the circumstances that come our way, but we do have a choice over the way we respond. When we choose to be positive, it's amazing what we end up rejoicing over.

"I spent the next five days in the hospital," Josh says, "and there was great rejoicing on day four when I regained flatulence. Praise the Lord for flatulence! This was key to my recovery, because it was the first tangible sign that my body was able to regain its ability to function outside of heavy medication."

Another immediate benefit to the surgery was that Josh instantly grew three-quarters of an inch, which is a big deal when you are shorter than most of your peers. The surgery corrected the curvature to a livable 37 degrees, which gave Josh the opportunity to engage in soccer, weight lifting, and pole vaulting within 12 months of the surgery.

Waiting gets us ready. Waiting is one of life's most strategic skills. It prepares in us the character we need to accomplish our best feats, and it positions us to be in the right place at the right time. Looking back, we are either glad we waited or we regret that we didn't wait.

In the midst of life, however, waiting seems to be torture. We get frustrated that we cannot make things happen faster, and we begin to feel we are victims rather than conquerors. It's all too easy to reach the conclusion that nothing will happen, or the wrong thing will happen, if we don't jump in and do something about it.

In reality, waiting prepares us for our greatest moments. God knows when we have developed the character and skills necessary for the next venture, so He has us wait. We think we are ready sooner, so we get in a hurry. God has us wait. We think that circumstances are moving too slow, so we get in a hurry. God has us wait. We are greatly concerned about the outcome of our lives, so we get in a hurry. But our impatience opposes what God is trying to do through us. So when you are waiting, thank God for the wait because it means He is investing in you.

Josh's New Pursuit

Most importantly, Josh's capacity for life has increased so that he can carry more responsibility and feel less stress. "In the buildup to and the aftermath of the surgery, I took comfort in Psalm 40, especially the first three verses:

> I waited patiently for the LORD;
>   he turned to me and heard my cry.
> He lifted me out of the slimy pit,
>   out of the mud and mire;

> he set my feet on a rock
>> and gave me a firm place to stand.
> He put a new song in my mouth,
>> a hymn of praise to our God.
> Many will see and fear
>> and put their trust in the LORD.

"It is fair to say that in the throes of the post-surgery unmedicated and unmitigated pain, I was impatient. But at the same time, He heard my cry, and He used my surgery and largely bed-ridden days of recovery to allow me to reflect on my priorities as a young man of 16. It made me realize how petty my worries and desires were, how very blessed I was, and how my attitude and treatment of people had to change."

Josh's Advice

"Roll with the punches. Optimism is a wonderful attribute that makes life livable in the worst of times and far more enjoyable in the best of times. As Christians, our belief in the gospel allows us to be optimistic and hopeful for things to come. It can certainly be a struggle to be an optimist when setbacks and disappointments disrupt our life, but God is in control. We can roll with the punches because He is in the ring with us, and with Him on our side, we cannot be knocked out of the fight. I believe this is the point of Proverbs 3:5-6,

> Trust in the LORD with all your heart
>> and lean not on your own understanding;
> in all your ways acknowledge him,
>> and he will make your paths straight."

Josh is fortunate because he learned early the value of active waiting. When we met Josh, we were impressed with his maturity and leadership. He is still actively waiting to see if God will allow him to marry and how God might introduce that special someone into his life. He is waiting to see if his military service will keep him in the States or send him overseas. He is waiting to see how God will send him new friends in every place he might be stationed. He is waiting to see just how his desire for ministry will be coupled with his desire to serve his country and serve the law.

He has learned that waiting is always part of the equation. He entered law school because he recognized he had talent in this area. He was, however, not sure this was exactly what he wanted to do. He attended classes and did his work while he prayed for wisdom to know what God wanted. After his second year, he strongly considered quitting law school to enter the ministry. He prayed fervently, deliberated over his options, sought counsel from various people he respected, and finally interviewed with the Army JAG Corps field screening officer.

He developed a strong sense that his future included JAG Corps, but he had to wait even more because he faced the possibility that his spinal fusion would eliminate this option. After a subsequent physical in October 2008, he was medically disqualified. As a matter of routine, his file went before the medical review board. While Josh waited, he prayed, and by God's grace, a waiver was granted.

While he waited, he also needed to stay in shape. So Josh did sit-ups, which he continues to do in his unique way as he pursues his profession as a lawyer in the Army.

"Prior to surgery, when performing a sit-up, I, like anyone, could curl my back a good deal prior to utilizing my abdomen and hip-flexor muscles to complete the sit-up. I no longer have that ability with my back. Instead, for me it's now almost 100 percent abdomen and hip flexors. Who knows, I might inspire others to do *flat-back Josh-ups*. I'll have to wait to see if it catches on!"

We're not sure if Josh's version of the sit-up will catch on, but we hope his courage and commitment do.

Just for fun

Doing the right thing while waiting can sometimes go too far, as Lorna and her friend found out:

My new friend, Lorna, was in front of me at the Tesco Extra supermarket checkout. She had written a check for her purchases and was waiting for the cashier to complete the transaction.

The cashier was a fine-looking young man named Richard, and he asked Lorna for proof of identity, citing "company policy."

Lorna was flabbergasted. Eventually she managed to squeak, "But Richard, I'm your mother."[1]

CHAPTER 6

Decide to Define Relationships

"The fruit of the Spirit is...kindness."

Galatians 5:22

Relationships can be exciting, thrilling, exhilarating—and frustrating, annoying, heartbreaking, and unpredictable. For example, one woman shared this story:

> My grandmother told me how she ended up marrying Grandpa. She was in her twenties, and the man she was dating left for war.
>
> "We were in love," she recalled, "and wrote to each other every week. It was during that time that I discovered how wonderful your grandfather was."
>
> "Did you marry Grandpa when he came home from the war?" I asked.
>
> "Oh, I didn't marry the man who wrote the letters. Your grandfather was the mailman."

Given that the heart is fickle, and emotions run deep like the ocean and strong like the wind, how can one truly be kind when it comes to the hearts of others? How can you create a circle of healthy relationships and forge a healthy life? DEFINE your relationships! All healthy relationships, in friendship and in love, are defined. Let's work through a simple acrostic that will help you understand the process that makes for healthy relationships:

Determine commitment level

Evaluate the environment

Fine-tune boundaries

Invest in self-care

Network for success

Enhance your goodbyes

Determine Commitment Level

Every healthy relationship contains two elements: two healthy people and one well-communicated commitment level. Both parties need to know the level of their relationship, and all expressions of affection—all gifts and all interactions—should match what is appropriate at that level.

Emotional lines can get blurry in friendship and work relationships too. How much do you confide in a coworker, a boss, or a friend? At what point do you trust a person with personal information? When or why would a person ever loan money or ask for a loan? When would a person comment on clothes or behaviors of another? Who do you allow to "friend" you on Facebook or follow you on Twitter, and what should or shouldn't you tweet or share on Facebook?

Relationships involve so many decisions, perhaps a few signposts should be set in place as a safeguard in sharing yourself with others. Here's how to play it SAFE:

Share incrementally

Always have an escape hatch

Find the forward movement

Evaluate favors carefully

Share Incrementally

Let relationships evolve as you lay a foundation of trust. Do not give out a lot of personal information when you first meet someone. If they ask,

"Where do you live?" say the city or area, not the street. If they Facebook "friend you," ask how they know you and find out the link between your friendship circles before you okay them. Look for safe ways to share more if you have interest in developing a friendship: be involved in the same Bible studies, charity causes, volunteer activities, or hobbies with groups of people first, then slowly evolve into smaller social circles with the person such as a smaller dinner party or a group date with friends. Then consider a double date to evaluate your comfort level before you share a solo dating experience.

Always Have an Escape Hatch

We live in a crazy world, so it is prudent to drive to and from your dates until you have thoroughly checked out a person. So how do you check out someone? A background check through a private detective? That's a thorough option, but it could get expensive if you date often. For the average person, you can do your own research:

- What is their online presence?
  - What are they writing on their Facebook or Twitter accounts?
  - Who are their friends and what kind of conversations are they having?
  - Are they being recognized in a positive way on their workplace website?
  - Are they on any watch lists? You can check to see if they are a sex offender at www.sexualoffenders.com.
- What are their work relationships like?
  - Do you know anyone from the company where they work?
  - Do you know their employment history and highlights?
- What is their social and family circle?
  - Are they close to their family and have you met any family members?

- Who are their friends and are you comfortable with them?
- Where do they spend their off-work time?
- Do they seem to have any friends they do not want you to meet?

• What is their financial status?

- Are they living within their means or are they stressed by debt?
- Have school loans been repaid?
- Do they use credit more than you feel comfortable with?

• How are they handling responsibility?

- Do they work? And how hard?
- Do they abuse or frequently use alcohol, drugs, or tobacco?
- How clean is their car? (or later, how clean is their home, patio, or yard?)
- How is their personal hygiene?

Even after you have a clearer picture of the person you are dating or socializing with, it's good early in the relationship to drive your own car to an event or date. You always want an escape if things go awry.

Find the Forward Movement

Often people in close friendships get stuck in unhealthy patterns. Many of the women I (Pam) talk to express frustration over male friends they cooked, cleaned house, or even did laundry for, but that person just saw them as a friend, not dating material. If you are doing the tasks of a husband or wife but there is no romantic interest, you are likely setting yourself up for some hurt. While it might be helpful to have friends who share their talents and skills in a give-and-take way, be cautious if all you do is *give* and all they do is *take*.

Maybe your grandmother reminded you of good moral choices with this familiar refrain: "Why should they buy the cow when they can get the milk for free?" This usually was spoken in the context of giving away your sexuality, but it can also be extended to when you do things a spouse would do without forward movement in the relationship. If you find it helpful to exchange talents, make it clear that you are giving this in exchange for something, or you are giving it as a gift because Jesus asked you to.

It's fine to give away your time, talent, or treasures if it truly is a gift freely given not a gift given in hopes that it will buy you into the heart of another. Make sure the agreements are clearly communicated if you want the commitment level of the relationship to be clear.

Evaluate Favors Carefully

When it comes to income, singles grasp the harsh reality, "We are on our own!" There is no sugar daddy funding your dream—or at least there shouldn't be. It isn't emotionally healthy to depend on someone else's money to pay your way in life. Money always comes with strings—there will always be payment required—of some kind.

Sarah found this out the hard way. Young, beautiful but a struggling grad student, she began to date a 40-something man. He was successful and lavished her with gifts, paid her tuition, moved her into his luxurious home—all with the clear expectation of sexual favors. At first she felt a sense of relief, but soon he became more demanding, more controlling, and her lavish lifestyle felt like nothing more than high-class prostitution. She wanted out, but getting out wasn't as easy as getting in. Her "boyfriend" kept her on a short leash, so she knew she would have to be creative to get out. One day when he was at a business meeting, she packed up her suitcases and left.

When I (Pam) met her, she told me, "I am poorer in my bank account but richer in self-esteem. God is walking me through and getting me to a better place. I learned there are no shortcuts in life. I feel better about me and about life since I'm earning my own way."

John was also taken in by what he thought was a benefactor for his artwork. This older woman seemed to believe in his work and wanted to help him launch his own line of art. However, she soon began to express a desire to take him places in her social circle. At first he enjoyed the luxury of lunches at nice clubs and restaurants, but when he mentioned that he needed to leave for a date one day, his benefactor went ballistic. She ranted that he was to be at her side, not someone else's, since she had invested so much in him.

Favors can turn into strings very quickly, sometimes without you knowing the rules have changed. This principle should extend to gifts you accept from your dates' friends and family. If it's a high-ticket item, that person might pressure your dating relationship to be at a higher commitment level than you desire. You can feel obligated to keep dating someone just because everyone in that person's world has been so nice to you. So be careful when accepting gifts that might leverage you right into the family. Every favor, every gift, every minute you spend with someone creates an emotional bond, so the more serious the relationship becomes, the harder it is to walk away from that person without causing pain to them—or to you.

It's like a spider and a web. When a spider catches its prey in its web, the spider continues to spin a web that further entraps its prey. If you want to be caught by the person you are dating, this is a good thing. All those connections build a stronger and stronger web around your love. The cocoon will be around the two of you, and it will be wonderful and strong. But if you are not ready for a close, committed relationship but you accept gifts and favors and spend all kinds of time with a person, it will be painful when you leave.

Jer had been dating Claire for a couple years, and their relationship was getting serious. Jer was in graduate school, so Claire's family and friends offered him furniture for his apartment, which he accepted. On his birthday, her parents gave him a gift that cost several hundred dollars. The birthday gift his family gave Claire was a much less expensive, friendship-level present. When Jer began to have car trouble, Claire's family offered to sell their car to Jer significantly below blue book with payments that could be repaid "whenever you have the money."

All this seemed very generous until Jer began to notice that invitations to events involving family were more like edicts than invitations. It began to feel as though there were more than two people in the dating relationship because the will of Claire's mom and dad and the extended family always determined how Jer and Claire spent their time. The more gifts

Claire's family gave, the more they criticized Jer. What once looked like favors and gracious gifts began to be used against him.

"I couldn't take it anymore," Jer said. "Every comment was negative, and the list of expectations and demands was getting longer and longer. I had thought Claire was the woman I wanted to marry. When I realized I was marrying her family too, I couldn't picture a lifetime of negative comments and an ever-growing list of orders and demands. I should have gone with my gut early on when the first expensive gift was offered. I should have declined it. Sometimes I would feel uncomfortable with their gifts or their offers for help, but Claire would say, 'They love you. They want to do this.'

"That might have been true. In their way I'm sure they did love me, but it came with too high a tab, too large a bill, and too many strings. Next time I'll make sure I'm very careful deciding what I receive and when I receive it, because nothing in life is really free. Everything has a price tag. It's just sometimes you don't know what it will cost or when that bill will come due."

Evaluate the Environment

Some people are toxic and create a toxic environment wherever they go. In the Charlie Brown cartoon strip, Pig-Pen never takes a bath. A dirt cloud surrounds him everywhere he travels. Real people can be like this too. Picture life as a coffee cup. Pain builds up, and when it reaches the top, the pain spills over and splashes on whoever is near. The toxic waste of some people's emotional cup sloshes out and poisons those in their world, even those they may love. Coffee cups are made for carrying coffee, not toxic waste, and people are created to be vessels of love, not emotional poison.

Some people are just not ready to be in a relationship because they are not willing to deal with their personal poison. Toxicity can come in many forms. Some people always find the glass half empty so that negativity is their first response. Others have a sarcastic slice to their tongue, tearing people apart with their words. Some have no self-control, so their addictions ruin the calm and peace of everyone connected to them. Others are so self-absorbed and narcissistic that if things don't go their way, it is always drama. Still others control through intimidation, using such tactics as physical and verbal abuse or suicidal threats so people around them are run by fear or guilt. The list of unhealthy choices is a long one.

If a characteristic of a healthy relationship is loving as God loves, then a toxic relationship would be characterized by the opposite of that love. Let's rewrite the familiar 1 Corinthians 13 passage on love as if Satan had turned it inside out and backwards.

> Toxic is impatient and unkind. Toxic is always envious and jealous. Toxic boasts and is self-glorifying. Toxic is arrogant and proud, self-centered and rude. Toxic easily loses its temper and keeps track of all offenses and holds a grudge. Toxic is thrilled when people look and feel stupid. Toxic loves a mistake because she can tell everyone of the error and replay it over and over. Toxic runs to evil, never protects others, and gives up on people and life easily.

Toxic would poison the Golden Rule and turn it into, *Do unto others before they do it to you. Exploit others before they exploit you.* And it would scoff at Jesus' example of sacrificing for others. Instead, toxic would sacrifice others for its own benefit or entertainment.

Toxic is just what it sounds like: a place to dump poison, hazardous waste, dangerous toxins, and life-killing sewage. Jesus comes to give life abundantly, the thief (Satan) comes to kill, steal, and destroy (John 10:10). If someone is killing your hopes, dreams, and self-esteem, if they are stealing your future, your safety, or your money, if they are destroying your reputation, your peace of mind, or your property—chances are they are toxic!

If you leave someone's presence and you feel closer to God, that is healthy. If you feel like Satan has just worked you over, that is a toxic person. One can minister to a toxic person, but you are on dangerous ground if you date or marry one. It will even be hard to be close friends with someone if they are toxic and unwilling to get help for their inner pain.

Leslie Vernick, author of *Emotionally Destructive Relationships*, gives this test to help you know when a relationship becomes destructive:

1. One or both parties commit physical, emotional, verbal, or sexual abuse upon the other.

2. One person is regularly overprotective, overbearing, or both toward the other.

3. One person is overly dependent upon the other to affirm his or her personal value and worth, to meet all of his or her needs, and to make most of his or her decisions.

4. One person demonstrates a pattern of deceiving the other through lying, hiding, pretending, misleading, or twisting information to make something appear other than what it is.

5. One person exhibits chronic indifference, neglect, or both toward thoughts, feelings, or well-being of the other.[1]

Leslie is a licensed clinical social worker, so helping people deal with toxic relationships has become an area of expertise. She learned first, however, by having to deal with members of her own dysfunctional family of origin. In a nutshell, Leslie shares how she dealt with her toxic person and how you can deal with your toxic person in an easy to remember three-step process. The process is Leslie's, but we have summarized it in our own words:

Speak up. Voice your hurt, pain, or discomfort to the person who is hurting you. When someone explains their hurt, pain, or frustration to a healthy person, that person will want to fix the relationship and find some kind of win-win. A toxic person will dismiss your pain. Develop a plan for how you will respond if a toxic person continues to hurt you. If they continue, then you will…

Stand up. If the person continues their destructive behaviors, explain to them the consequences. If they still continue to hurt you, then you will…

Step back. Pull away from the relationship far enough to feel safe. Follow through on the natural consequences you explained previously. Set boundaries in place to protect the remnant of the relationship and give God time to work to heal that person—and to heal your heart and hurts.

Fine-Tune Boundaries

Having relationship standards and boundaries keeps a relationship honest. When the cards are laid on the table early, people know what to expect. But in order to explain your personal standards, you have to first have some! In an age of friends with benefits, sugar daddies, and a media filled with porn, promiscuity, profanity, and a preoccupation with sex, it is necessary to create your own inner compass. The only way to protect your heart is to verbalize your standards to your friends and romantic interests.

The Things We Do for Love

Let's take a quick look at sex from God's point of view. In *Red-Hot Monogamy*, we give five reasons for God creating sex within marriage:

- Procreation—It's how God chose to populate the human race.

- Recreation—It's fun when it is expressed in the safety of a committed marriage.

- Regeneration—It produces endorphins that keep us healthy (when expressed inside marriage, which limits the negative side effects such as STDs).

- Reconnection—It keeps married couples cemented together even in rough times.

- Proclamation—When a married couple has a strong relationship, it reflects God's love.

In the same way, when you as a single handle your sexuality with responsibility, you too reflect God's glory. God's goal for relationships is to protect and provide for people so that communities, churches, and families are strong and stable. Hooking up, friends with benefits, sex with a multitude of partners, sexting, pornography, or even sex with one person outside the context of marriage does not protect nor provide.

Want to See God?

In the beatitudes, Jesus said, "Blessed are the pure in heart for they shall see God" (Matthew 5:8). Picture sexuality as a continuum. At one end is holding hands; sexual intercourse and oral sex are at the other end. We know from 1 Thessalonians 4:3 that it is God's will for you to abstain from sexual immorality (which means any sex outside marriage). So God knows that to stay pure in heart, you have to set your boundaries before oral sex and intercourse occur. But how far back from that do you need to push the line to maintain your ability to "see God" or maintain your pure heart and protect the purity of those you date?

If sexual intercourse is out of God's will until marriage, then the things that prepare your body to give and receive sex are a dangerous, slippery slope. Stimulating sexual organs under clothes or over clothes is a part of the sexual dance. It makes sense that the line of purity should be drawn before sexual foreplay.

But how far back before this should your line be? For some, making out sets them up to desire sexual intercourse. Others seem to think they can handle extended making-out and kissing sessions and not fall into sexual temptation. The majority of people, though, long for more and more and keep pushing the envelope once make-out sessions begin. So move the line back.

Some can handle a good night kiss or a greeting kiss. Some can kiss after prayer together and maintain a pure heart. Still others will find that any kissing, even one, lights the fires of passion. The key to success is to get to know yourself so you can wisely set your personal boundaries. Most people fail because they are not honest *with themselves*, let alone honest with the person they are dating.

Doctors Joe S. McIlhaney Jr. and Freda McKissic Bush have written *Hooked,* a book on how sex affects our brains. The good doctors describe sex as "any intimate contact between two individuals that involves arousal, stimulization, and/or a response by at least one of the two partners."[2] Basically, intimate contact *at some point* shifts to acquiring *the purpose and intention* of sexual intercourse. What is your purpose? What is your intention? Draw a heart symbol on the sexual-intimacy continuum below where you would need to limit your level of intimacy to maintain a pure heart. Now draw a star where your intent changes from romance to sexual response.

How far am I willing to go?

✓ Set the line prior to intercourse (1 Thessalonians 4:3)
✓ Push the line back as far as you need to maintain purity
(Matthew 5:8)

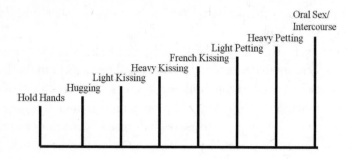

Your heart should precede the star. For example, if heavy kissing makes you desire sex (the star mark), then give yourself a margin and mark light kissing with the heart. We all need a margin to safeguard our heart and life.

We want to be up front here. Approximately 70 percent of singles have had at least one sexual experience outside of marriage, but the people who say sex is most fulfilling (and have it more frequently) are long-term married couples. Sex as a single just comes with too many risks, including the risk that your partner will hurt you or abandon you. Here are a few more, according to the United States surgeon general:

- Sexually transmitted diseases (STDs) infect approximately 12 million Americans each year.

- An estimated 40,000 new HIV infections occur each year.

- An estimated 1.37 million induced abortions occur yearly.

- Nearly one-half of pregnancies are unintended.

According to the U.S. Centers for Disease Control and Prevention (CDC), STDs are a rising epidemic in our nation, with some 65 million Americans plagued with an incurable form. [3]

It is hard to enjoy an experience that has such a high potential for ripping your heart and life in two. No matter your past, now is the time to decide your future. Giving yourself a margin will safeguard your future.

What Science Has to Say

There is a reason why sexual integrity is so difficult. McIlhaney and Bush explain that when something makes you feel good, "dopamine rewards us by flooding our brains and making the brain cells produce a feeling of excitement or of well-being...it makes us feel the need or desire to repeat pleasurable, exciting, and rewarding acts...It should be noted, however, that dopamine is values-neutral. In other words, it is an involuntary response that cannot tell right from wrong."[4] The doctors continue to explain that sex is one of the strongest generators of dopamine, so people are "vulnerable to falling into a cycle of dopamine reward for unwise sexual behavior—they can get hooked on it."[5]

In addition, in the female brain, oxytocin, another neurochemical that creates bonding, is also kicked off in sex. It becomes like superglue, but again it is values neutral. This bonding chemical accumulates so that a person is drawn to stay with a person because of their sexual relationship even if that person is seen as undesirable in other areas—even if they might be abusive or possessive or otherwise dysfunctional. Oxytocin can cause a person to feel that their sexual partner is trustworthy even if he or she is not!

But it is not just the women who can experience this irrational bonding through sex. Vasopressin in men creates a similar bonding experience. This bonding is created by God to enhance marital stability, but for singles it can cause a person to attach to someone who might not be healthy for them.

If a man decides he does not want to be in a committed relationship, but he's addicted to the dopamine rush that sex creates, he might go from partner to partner. This action can "cause his or her brain to mold and gel so that it eventually begins to accept this sexual pattern as normal...The pattern of changing sex partners therefore seems to damage their ability to bond in a committed relationship."[6] Dave Carder in *Close Calls* contends that the relationship stops growing when it becomes sexual because the primary focus of the couple's time together becomes sex.[7]

Sex Is Hot, Disease Is Not

More than 70 million Americans are living with sexually transmitted diseases. About 19 million more are diagnosed every year, the majority under age 25.[8] "Today there are more than twenty-five sexually transmitted infections worthy of serious concern. Most of these diseases are viral, and though there are drugs to suppress some of them, none of the viral ones can be cured." One in every four teens is infected.[9] "The rates of many STDs, including gonorrhea, genital herpes, and human papillomavirus (HPV), continue to rise rapidly. In addition, the viral chlamydia trachomatis is connected to pelvic inflammatory disease, which is the fastest growing cause of infertility. STDs, in fact, are a direct cause of infertility in both men and women, and an estimated 95 percent of cervical cancer cases are associated with HPV."[10]

One of the most heartbreaking moments of my ministry occurred when I (Pam) was speaking at an event for mothers. One mom and several small children came up to me after my "Red-Hot Monogamy" talk aimed at married women. In tears she said,

> My marriage isn't red hot. It can't be because before I married, I slept with someone other than my husband, and he gave me herpes. Now my entire married life is impacted because a person from my past dictates when I can be with my husband. Every outbreak reminds me of my mistake. Every outbreak reminds me that I gave my heart and my body to someone who in turn gave me a disease. Apart from a miracle of science, I will never get rid of this anchor around my marriage.

The consequences of sexually transmitted diseases range from pain to sterility to cancer to death (from HIV/AIDS). The average orgasm lasts only about 90 seconds and the average lovemaking session lasts less than an hour. How much of your future happiness do you want to gamble for a few moments of dopamine rush?[11]

Commitment Is Cool

What causes sex to be fulfilling is trust. When doing research for our first book, *Pure Pleasure*, we discovered that the number one indicator that released a woman to enjoy the sexual experience was her ability to trust the one making love to her. Commitment, like the kind found in a marriage where two people have made vows before God and their friends and family, provides the safety net that creates such a trusting environment.

Barbara Wilson, author of *The Invisible Bond: How to Break Free from Your Sexual Past*, was invited to the United Nations to share her expertise. Barbara concurs that the majority of those who experience sex outside of marriage are disappointed and even harmed:

> I've discovered after leading hundreds of women through sexual healing that their first sexual experience outside marriage is seldom what they expected. In many cases it's forced, unplanned, hurried and not sexually satisfying…Even more, the negative associations with that first sexual experience can follow them into their marriages, causing them to shut down physically and robbing them of the kind of intimacy God desires for them in marriage. And it's not just my experience. Studies show that most young people wished they'd waited to have sex. According to the National Campaign to Prevent Teen Pregnancy, 55 percent of sexually active [males], and 72 percent of sexually active [women] under age 20 said they wished they'd have waited to have sex.[12]

The Living Together Phenomenon

So perhaps you're thinking, "Well, then I won't sleep around. I'll just sleep with the person I'm with, and we can just move in together until we decide to marry. Marriage is just a piece of paper, right?" This might be a good line of reasoning except for a few compelling facts:

- Sex in a live-in relationship is still sex that can bond you to an unhealthy person. If you have had many sexual partners prior to living with this one, then your brain is still patterned to love and leave. Living together rather than making the commitment of marriage just reinforces the "back door is always open" thinking that can destroy love.

- The majority of cohabiting couples describe their relationship as "on the rocks."[13]

- Couples who cohabited before they married are twice as likely to divorce compared to those who did not live together prior to marriage.

- Cohabiting couples are more prone to domestic violence.

- Cohabiting couples are four times more likely to cheat on their partner than those who marry.[14]

- Cohabiting couples are more likely to produce children, and this can place undue stress on a relationship that is yet to be rooted and strengthened.

- Cohabiting couples' love is temporary. Only one in six will stay together three years, and only one in ten will last ten years or more. Most cohabiting couples last a mere 18 months.[15]

It has been our experience as pastors and relationship specialists that the majority of people who enter a live-in relationship do not end up getting married. A few do, and a few of those stay married, but they are defying the odds. The majority of the cohabiting couples we see spend a few years with a person and then move on. Sometimes women wait years for their live-in boyfriend to propose, and most never do. Then the woman realizes she has given away some of the best years of her life and a good portion of her heart to someone who didn't love her enough to commit to her and her future. Sometimes the man in a live-in situation wants to marry his partner, but she is afraid of marriage for some reason. He feels his future is in a holding pattern, just circling the airport unable to land.

Living together is counterproductive to long-term love for at least the following reasons:

1. You are deciding together to disobey God. This is not a great start or a strong foundation to build on.

2. You are deciding to not decide on the key issue that moves your future forward. Are you willing to place all your eggs in this relationship basket, knowing that your partner could move to another city, to another partner, to another residence at a moment's notice? Cohabitation by definition is unstable

and insecure, so your life can change overnight. Moving out is not the same as divorce. Divorce proceedings at least hold out the possibility that such things as division of property and alimony will help stabilize a person during the trauma of the end of a relationship.

3. Cohabiting is not a good test for compatibility. Living with a back door open, an escape hatch, an exit plan, is not the same as marriage.

If testing the relationship is the goal, cohabitation will not help you discern it in a realistic way.

Invest in Self-Care

Since we are talking about sexuality, we have to deal with a common issue for singles: masturbation. Almost everyone wonders about this but not very many talk about. It's no secret that we are all sexual beings. We all have sexual organs, we all have sexual thoughts, and we all have to decide how and when we will express ourselves sexually. Therefore, one of the most important questions we need to answer is, "How am I going to handle the sexual drive God has created in me?" This question has many versions depending on your current season of life and your current relational involvement:

- If I am not in a relationship and my sexual drive is strong, what am I supposed to do?

- If I am in a relationship and I'm trying to maintain integrity toward my partner so that we're not having sex outside marriage, how do I process my sexual thoughts and urges?

- Is it ever okay to give myself sexual release? If so, when would that be?

- Will masturbation protect me from stepping across the line into fornication (sexual immorality prior to marriage)?

- What does God think about self-stimulation?

Amazingly, the Bible says nothing directly about masturbation. In order to answer our questions, we need to examine the principles that apply rather look for a "thou shalt" or "thou shalt not."

Avoid the Ridiculous

Throughout history there have been sincerely motivated but ridiculous notions about masturbation. Cold showers might shock you out of the mood, but they do not extinguish your sex drive. You will not go blind if you masturbate. You will not go insane. And you will not necessarily lose your interest in a healthy romantic relationship.

Did you know there's a historical connection between masturbation, graham crackers, and cornflakes?

> In 1834 Dr. Sylvester Graham wrote that the loss of semen during sex was injurious to health (a popular idea at the time); men, Graham believed, should not have intercourse more than twelve times a year. Masturbation was especially pernicious, he said. To reduce sexual cravings, Graham advised mild foods to decrease sexual appetites. The graham cracker was the result! In 1884, this curious connection between food and sex appeared in another guise. Dr. John Harvey Kellogg created cornflakes to curtail children's inclinations toward masturbation.[16]

So our advice—cold showers with a graham cracker and cornflake diet. (Just kidding!)

We are pretty sure cornflakes and graham crackers are not the real answer to this dilemma. If you are going to reach a rational, realistic conclusion about your private sexual behavior, you will want to leave the ridiculous notions about masturbation out of the conversation.

Get Smart

The human sex drive is one the most mysterious and relentless aspects of life. Women are drawn to being emotionally, romantically, and socially connected. They dream about it as little girls and long for it as adults. History is filled with both sentimental and sad stories of women who have sacrificed deeply just to be in a relationship. If not kept in check, this desire to be connected can shatter common sense and override natural inhibitions. Men are driven to release the semen that regularly builds up in their bodies. High levels of testosterone cause men to think about sex often and to respond to almost any visual stimulation. Left unchecked, this physical desire will obliterate moral values and override normal restraint.

As we mentioned before, powerful chemicals are involved with any sexual expression, which makes this an intense struggle in our lives. Maintaining your sexual purity, therefore, requires you to be alert and sober minded.

> Let us not be like others, who are asleep, but let us be alert and self-controlled (1 Thessalonians 5:6).

> Be self-controlled and alert. Your enemy the devil prowls around like a roaring lion looking for someone to devour (1 Peter 5:8).

For you to remain sexually pure, therefore, will take more than a casual decision. Rather, it will take a sober-minded, alert-to-danger, conscientious choice.

Guilt Is Not Your Friend

It's safe to say that most people think masturbation should either be avoided completely or practiced rarely. We doubt anyone would say, "I think masturbation is one of the spiritual disciplines. It helps me grow closer to Jesus and think clearer about all my decisions." More commonly what we hear is, "This is such a struggle for me. At times it seems to help, but I don't think it's something I should be doing." One woman online represented this viewpoint well:

> I became a widow one-and-a-half years ago. My husband and I loved making love. It was so wonderful to show each other how much we loved each other, and it was something only the two of us shared. Now he is gone, and I long for him and I have dreamt of him while pleasing myself. I feel very close to him when I do it, but then I feel guilty that I was not pleasing to God. I don't do it often, maybe once a month, but this has bothered me ever since my husband passed away. The love I have for him is still as strong as it always was. Is there any exceptions????[17]

We would never recommend that you take the boundaries off and masturbate anytime you want, but we also do not encourage you to wallow in guilt. Responsive guilt that motivates us to repent from poor decisions is a good thing, but chronic guilt can become a destructive force that causes people to become self-absorbed, self-centered, and self-destructive. Jesus died to free us from our guilt, and He calls us to walk in grace. When we regularly dwell on feeling guilty rather than confessing our sins and accepting God's forgiveness, we fight against the growth He is trying to accomplish in us.

- Guilt focuses us on our shortcomings.
  Grace focuses on God's power.

- Guilt causes us to feel bad about ourselves.
  Grace causes us to feel good about God.

- Guilt leads us to meditate on our mistakes.
  Grace leads us to meditate on God's truth.

- Guilt drives us to despise our imperfections.
  Grace drives us to be amazed at God's creation.

- Guilt steals energy.
  Grace energizes us with purpose.

The goal then is to set your convictions in a way that helps you stay focused on God's grace. Included in the plan should be a way to recover quickly when you don't live up to your own standards. Your recovery plan should definitely include confession (1 John 1:9), which involves an admission that you violated your convictions, thankfulness that you have been forgiven, and a request for God to fill you with the Holy Spirit (Ephesians 5:18). Another step we have found helpful was introduced to us by our mentor, Jim Conway. He showed us Galatians 5:16, "walk by the Spirit, and do not gratify the desires of the flesh," and then recommended that we pray, "Jesus, please meet the need in my life that I think this activity (or person) will meet." This type of honest prayer helps you shift your thoughts to Jesus rather than focusing on the thing you wished you hadn't done.

Seek Excellence

The goal of our lives on earth is not perfection, since we will wrestle with our old nature until the day we see Jesus face-to-face. We are, however, called to live with excellence. "For the grace of God that brings salvation has appeared to all men. It teaches us to say 'No' to ungodliness and worldly passions, and to live self-controlled, upright and godly lives in this present age" (Titus 2:11-12). Notice that grace teaches us to say no to some things and yes to others. Paul is reminding Titus, and all of us, that when we are free, it is best to live free.

So how do we live with excellence when it comes to sexual expression?

Excellence guards the heart and mind. The real battle over sexual purity takes place in the inner man. Jesus clearly proclaimed this in Matthew 5:28, "But I tell you that anyone who looks at a woman lustfully has already committed adultery with her in his heart." A person guilty of this offense hasn't done anything but think, and yet Jesus says that his heart is affected by what he entertained in his mind. The apostle Paul echoes the notion that victory is won in the mind when he wrote, "whatever is true, whatever is noble, whatever is right, whatever is pure, whatever is lovely, whatever is admirable—if anything is excellent or praiseworthy—think about such things" (Philippians 4:8).

We believe this is where the biggest struggle exists. We live in a world that feeds our minds incessantly with sexual messages. Pornography is the most obvious stimulus for immoral thinking, but it is certainly not the only one. Explicit movies, erotic commercials, novels, magazines, innuendos on TV shows, and comedians are all encouraging us to think about sex in a self-gratifying way. If you are going to think differently, you will be constantly rowing against the current. Self-stimulation becomes more difficult to resist when your mind is filled with sexual images or memories.

The real battle is in the mind, so any strategy for living with excellence must include a plan for regularly recharging your mind with truth.

Addictions Are Aggravating

The other conviction you will want to add to your list is an aggressive commitment to never accept addictive behavior. The powerful chemical processes that drive our sexual appetites have the potential to take over our lives and dominate our schedules. When this happens, any sexual activity, including masturbation, becomes an aggravatingly disappointing experience. Anytime an addiction establishes itself, it takes more and more stimulation to achieve the same response. What started out as a fun thing now becomes a cruel master that fails to deliver.

First Corinthians 6:12 draws us to the conclusion that we should never settle for being mastered by bad habits: "'Everything is permissible for me'—but not everything is beneficial. 'Everything is permissible for me'—but I will not be *mastered* by anything." When masturbation, or any other habit, begins to master or dominate your life, it is time to get help. When you plan your schedule around the opportunity to engage in an addictive experience, it is time to get help. When you lose the ability to say no to a behavior, it is time to get help.

Don't let anyone or anything except Jesus be the master of your life. Everything else will ultimately leave you empty, frustrated, and irritated. Only Jesus knows how to lead your life without taking away your freedom.

Network for Success

In relationships, trusting your network is a wise decision. No one knows you as well as your friends and family. If you want to battle loneliness, trust those closest to you when they say,

"You should try this Bible study."

"You might want to be a part of this group or volunteer for that cause."

"You should meet this person."

Those who love you have your best interests in mind.

When we surveyed singles, "the setup" was a common conversation. You know what we're talking about. You go to a social event and people say, "Oh, here's my friend so-and-so. You two will just love each other! Well, I gotta go. You two go ahead and talk." Awkward!

While most of those we surveyed felt uncomfortable with the obvious setup, the majority did like a responsible setup. Hosting a dinner where many people are invited with lots of possible friendship connections was generally accepted as a good idea. If you invite friends over and encourage them to invite friends, you can create a relaxed time together that fosters new, quality friendships. It's much more comfortable when you take advantage of natural friendship circles.

Broader social circles are also great networking environments. When you work or volunteer alongside other people, you get to know them under a little stress. Since stress tends to expose our character, working environments can be an effective way to determine who is healthy and who is not. This is why so many people develop lasting friendships or romantic interests at church and work.

A simple idea for expanding your social circle and that of your close friends is to host a party, a conference, or a service project where everyone invites three to five singles they know well and trust. Do not post an invitation on Facebook or distribute fliers or announce the event in front of a group. Do all the inviting through email or text messages or one-on-one conversations. If the dinner costs a little or the service project requires a donation, high-quality people will be attracted to the event. Add in some elbow grease, and people who are less committed will find other activities to keep them busy.

The goal of this type of gathering is to get the most responsible, hard-working, quality, purpose-driven singles to show up. They will not be coming to look for a date. They will come to serve with the natural byproduct of building friendships, and maybe a few nice dates will happen as well. Growing your social network in this way raises the bar on relationships.

Enhance Your Goodbyes

Many people have a psycho dating story. Often the most dramatic part of the story happens at the break-up phase. Jake realized after about four dates that Julie was just too high maintenance for him. His first clue might have been when she said, "I have my dad and granddad wrapped around my little finger. I can get them to do anything I want." Yep, flashing red light, and the Holy Spirit was probably screaming something like, "Run for your life!"

But Jake stayed a few dates longer.

Then one night, at the end of their date, he simply said, "This is not working for me, Julie. I just don't see us as compatible. I don't think we should date anymore."

Jake left and drove home, stopping at the store for the next day's food needs. When he arrived home, he walked into his room, and Julie was standing on his bed.

"You can't break up with me. I am not leaving until you tell me you will stay. You can't leave me!" She was clinging to him, sobbing and screaming.

Jake peeled himself away, then walked out to the entryway, propped open the door, and took out his cell phone. He then calmly said, "I'm sorry you feel this way. This is not the way to handle your feelings. Your actions have reinforced my decision to not date you. I am giving you a choice now. I can call the police and report you for breaking and entering, or you can calmly and quietly walk out of this place."

Jake's male roommate stood in the hallway with him for moral support.

It took a little while, but Julie finally said, "OK." Then she ran out of the apartment.

Yes, all singles need some equipping on "the breakup." Not every relationship is meant to develop into a lifelong friendship. Some people are friends for life, and others are friends for the road. Saying goodbye and learning to allow people out of your life is an important skill to develop. Most people are really bad at it. Saying, "It's not you, it's me," or "I just don't think of you that way," or "I don't want to ruin our friendship," might be a good attempt, but it's inadequate.

So what does a godly good breakup look like? How do you STOP dating someone?

Say clearly what this person has meant to you and how you value them. Then state as simply as possible that you want to cease dating the person. Don't beat around the bush. The person should clearly know that you want to end the relationship as it currently stands. They should also clearly know they are valued by God and are a valuable person, but they are just not the best fit for you. Often good people are just not good together.

Tactfully handle their feelings. Explain that you do not want to hurt them but that some of what you are saying might be hard to hear. Acknowledge their emotions. Hand them tissues, if necessary.

Openly explain the issues. It's only fair that you explain why you think this relationship isn't working. Sometimes a little training or some counseling can prepare someone for a bright relationship future. God might be using you as iron sharpening iron to better equip this person for more healthy relationships.

Prepare the new plan. Lay out what kind of relationship, friendship, working relationship you hope to have with him or her.

Relationships can be really complicated, but with a process that DEFINEs a relationship, life and love is less stressful and more enjoyable.

Just for fun

If you need advice, text me…

If you need a friend, call me…

If you need me, come to me…

If you need money…THE SUBSCRIBER CANNOT BE REACHED![18]

CHAPTER 7

Decide to Live the Good Life

"The fruit of the Spirit is...goodness."

GALATIANS 5:22

What is a good life? Country singers twang about it, poets wax eloquent describing it, and everyone is looking for it. But what is good? It's tough to define because we hold different definitions. What is good to one man is frightening to another. What seems good to one woman may seem reckless to another.

Even the Bible uses different words to talk about what is good. There are two general words, one which refers to things being useful while the other refers to things that are beautiful. There is also a fascinating word in 2 Peter 1:5 that is translated "goodness" and has the idea of morally heroic deeds. Figuring out what is good, therefore, is a pursuit of the heart that combines what is true with the creative variety God has expressed in us as individuals. So, what is good to you?

- Dark chocolate wrapped around ice cream?
- A warm latte on a cold day?
- Hand-squeezed, ice-cold lemonade on a scorching hot summer day?
- A gourmet meal cooked to perfection?
- A warm, steamy bath or shower after a killer workout?

- Fresh ocean air on a warm sandy beach—with plenty of shells?

- An unexpected raise or an unanticipated compliment or an unsolicited favor?

Perhaps good is the way you feel after a bike ride, a dance class, a run, or a paddle on a glassy lake. Maybe good is classical music soothing away your stress or melodic jazz that touches your soul or rock or metal that throbs in your eardrums. Good might be the way you are relaxed after a massage or the thrill of watching your favorite team win and the rush of celebrating with thousands of fans in a packed stadium. Good might be that perfect report card, glowing job review, or date with a new special someone. Good might be the sense of accomplishment after a job well done, or the sense of pride after completing that new work of art. Good might be the way you feel after a deep conversation with a dear friend or a memorable day with a parent, a niece, or sibling.

Good is, in one sense, very subjective because it is based on how we feel about our lives. Good doesn't stop there, however, because there is an objective side to what is good. Something that is destructive or harmful cannot be good, no matter how it feels. At minimum, something must be beautiful (in its own way), useful, and morally heroic to be considered good. For this reason, God is supremely good because He is more beautiful than anything He has made, more useful than any other being, and morally perfect. Since we are made in His image, we can reflect this goodness in our pursuits.

Well-Rounded Goodness

We have, over the years, had a number of experiences with bicycles. We have led bike trips for youth, used bikes instead of cars, and created some great friendship memories with our bicycles. One of the most important things we learned about bikes is that the wheels need to be "true" if we are going to enjoy the ride. This means the wheel must be adjusted so that the spokes are all at equal tension and the rim is actually round. If not, it produces a wobbly, bumpy ride.

Your life is the same way. If your major pursuits are balanced with each other, your life will be "true" and the path will be much easier to navigate. If not, you run the risk of a bumpy ride.

Your life is unique, so it will have unique commitments and pursuits that you must keep in balance. But there are a few areas of life that we must all address. These are the spokes of the wheel that provide the initial shape of your life. You are free to add spokes, but your life will work best if you are good at these vital areas. When life is out of balance, temptation intensifies as you consider shortcuts to getting your needs met. You can keep these spokes in balance by setting goals, searching out your aptitude, and designing a plan.

Who Wants to Be a Millionaire? Financial Goodness

Money is one of the great tools in life. In addition to survival needs, God has placed in the heart of each of us dreams that are funded by money. Therefore, if you are going to fulfill the plan God has for your life, you are going to have to be good with finances. The problem is that we all struggle to keep money in its proper balance.

The first part of the struggle is that we treat money as if it is more than a tool. We think it will bring happiness, companionship, and fulfillment—all the things relationships were designed to provide. As a result, many of us long to become rich, and the evidence is abundant in our world.

Patti Stanger is becoming rich and famous off her *The Millionaire Matchmaker* program on Bravo TV. Only millionaires, mostly male, are allowed into the prestigious club so they can select from over 30,000 potential mates. Patti claims that four out of five of the couples she puts together begin a relationship after their matchmaking experience. Her 30,000 clients are interested because they believe, "It's just as easy to fall in love and marry a rich man as a poor one." The popularity of riches is also evidenced by best-selling books such as *The Millionaire Next Door, The One Minute Millionaire,* and *Rich Dad Poor Dad*; magazines such as *Millionaire*; and TV shows such as *Who Wants to Be a Millionaire?* One source reported that 1 in every 125 Americans were millionaires in 2004—*before* the most recent stock market decline.[1]

But being a millionaire is still rare, and most people manage their financial journey by carrying debt rather than establishing sufficient cash flow. According to the American Debt Advisor website, 80 percent of adult Americans are in debt "if we include secured debts like homes and cars. Excluding those particular purchases puts us closer to 50% of the adult population, and half of that 50% has thousands of dollars owed."[2]

Stuart Vyse, author of *Going Broke: Why Americans Can't Hold On to Their Money*, estimates the numbers are even higher: "Today, the average American has more than $16,000 in debt, excluding mortgages."[3] Blogger Bob Lawless of Credit Slips points out the challenge this is creating—approximately 1 million bankruptcies were filed in the United States in 2008 followed by about 1.2 million in 2009. In 2009, the average was 5,075 filings each business day.[4]

We don't fault people for wanting to make a lot of money because it can be a very useful tool. We pray regularly that God will prosper His people so they can give money to ministries and charities that are helping people in need. The issue has never been the amount of money a person has. The real issue is the heart. Jesus said, "No one can serve two masters. Either he will hate the one and love the other, or he will be devoted to the one and despise the other. You cannot serve both God and Money" (Matthew 6:24). The apostle Paul echoed his Savior's words when he reminded us, "For the love of money is a root of all kinds of evil. Some people, eager for money, have wandered from the faith and pierced themselves with many griefs" (1 Timothy 6:10). He never said money is bad, but he did warn that loving money will corrupt the heart.

So what does it take to be good with money?

Set Financial Goals

We live in a world that is screaming for our attention. Buy a house, get a new phone, borrow to get a nicer car, wear newer clothes, get more entertainment options, and make sure you go somewhere exotic on vacation! These messages are being broadcast everyday in every possible way, and they are trying to capture your heart. The only way to see through the smokescreen of abundant possessions is to set goals that keep you focused.

Ellie Kay, author of *Living Rich for Less*, recommends if you are a single-income household that you set a goal of putting 12 months of living expenses in a liquid savings account. This goal has helped Ellie become a savings queen. She has ways to make a dollar stretch farther than spandex! Financial consultant Dave Ramsey, author of *Financial Peace*, encourages us all to set a goal of lowering debt so we can stop paying interest and start investing in the things we believe in.

You should focus on your income goals because you can't spend money unless you make money. How much money do you want to make? How productive do you want your career to be? How hard do you want to work? Do you want to work for someone else or do you want to run your own business? We know you can't force your goals to become a reality, but you can improve your effectiveness by choosing goals to guide your steps.

Search Out Your Financial Aptitude

Some people can handle large amounts of money without ever letting it get out of perspective. Others find anything beyond what they need too tempting to keep their hearts from wandering to self-destructive behaviors. A wise man by the name of Agur was keenly aware of this precipitous balance when he wrote:

> "Two things I ask of you, O LORD;
> do not refuse me before I die:
> Keep falsehood and lies far from me;
> give me neither poverty nor riches,
> but give me only my daily bread.
> Otherwise, I may have too much and disown you
> and say, 'Who is the LORD?'
> Or I may become poor and steal,
> and so dishonor the name of my God."
> (Proverbs 30:8-9)

Design a Financial Plan

Everyone who has ever set a goal has discovered that it is only a wish unless they develop a plan that helps them make progress toward the goal. A simple way Ellie Kay produces more spendable income is by using coupons, discounts, and bartering. If you are having trouble saving, consider enrolling in a few blog feeds so you gain easy access to coupons and specials, and put money-saving ideas right into your inbox.

If you have chronic debt, Dave Ramsey recommends a cash-only system that forces you to save for larger expense items instead of charging them. Part of the system includes a deliberate plan for paying off current debt, which includes a commitment to pay a little more than the minimum monthly payment on all forms of debt. Then choose the debt with the highest interest rate and pay as much as you can each month against that balance. If you repeat that process until all your debts are paid off, you'll be amazed at how quickly you can free yourself from the tyranny of constant debt. Crown Financial Ministries recommends that only a mortgage be carried as debt, and that you pay that off as rapidly as you can.

If these seem like overwhelming goals, just start with one step. Add a little to savings, whittle away on a debt. As you take action you will gain financial ground.

Take a moment and write down two financial goals, one that will produce more income and one that will reduce your expenses:

1.

2.

Heart Smart: Emotional Goodness

She was frantic to get ahold of me. She sent emails, made repeated cell calls, shot off tweets, Facebook messages, and texts. She needed to talk—now! She believed she had a one-of-a-kind problem, and she needed the best advice she could imagine. When she and I (Pam) finally connected, however, I heard the familiar refrain,

> I might have just lost the very best man I've ever known. I'm not sure what happened, but I think my baggage caught up with me. It's like some stranger took over my body. He hurt me—my feelings—so I unleashed. I hurt him back. I cried, I ranted, I just went ballistic! I stomped, threw stuff, I'm sure I broke some things. I swore—and I'm a Christian! I know better! What happened? Why would I do that? He called me and said he just can't handle my mood swings, my emotional outbursts. He can't handle high-maintenance me. I can't keep doing this. I can't handle high-maintenance me! I can't keep self-destructing.

The beat of your heart causes all the systems of your body to function, but unnatural rhythms create trauma that can interrupt routines and even end a life. In the same way, your life has an emotional rhythm that helps everything work well.

Set Emotional Goals

It seems almost too obvious to state, but goal number one is to develop a healthy emotional rhythm in your life. We believe emotional balance includes:

- *Laughter every day.* Proverbs 17:22 states, "A cheerful heart is good medicine, but a crushed spirit dries up the bones." Life is filled with humor, so it makes sense that a normal day will have moments of enjoyment that lead to laughter.

- *Appropriate reactions to life's circumstances.* Sometimes life is sad or sentimental, which leads to tears. Sometimes life is intense, which leads to focused determination. Sometimes life is relaxed, which leads to peaceful reflection. Emotional health gives us the ability to vary our reactions to the realities of life.

- *Managing stress to maintain productivity.* Some stress is necessary to keep us focused, while too much stress incapacitates us. The right amount of stress, therefore, keeps us energized and effective.

Search Out Your Emotional Capacity

Each of us has a unique limit to how much emotional input and expression we can handle. To find this limit, make commitments to friends, projects, and ministry activity until stress starts to make you ineffective. At that point, you will want to back off on your commitments until stress becomes manageable again. This is a lifelong process of adjustment that you will want to practice until it becomes a comfortable skill.

Unfortunately, many people have emotional arrhythmia created by wounds and past pains that sabotage their future. Georgia Shaffer, author of *Taking Out Your Emotional Trash*, attended a seminar by psychologist W. Robert Nay, a specialist in anger management.

> Many of the clients in his private practice were referred to him by the judicial system because their anger had gotten out of control. Dr. Nay said that when he speaks to these offenders about their feelings and what they noticed *before* they "lost it," they often said, "I was fine until that guy cut me off in traffic. I lost it *[they snap their fingers]* just like that."

Dr. Nay discovered no one loses it "just like that." Rather, the snap happens because a "cumulative force becomes so strong that when we experience one additional thing, even if it is something small…we snap."[5]

Design a Plan

We suggest you develop a plan to help you keep your expressions of emotion, especially your anger, under control.

First, practice laughing. Collect jokes, tell stories with friends, and watch entertainment that makes you smile. Deliberately find a way to laugh each day.

Next, get in the habit of asking, "Was my reaction to that situation appropriate?" If your reaction was good, thank God and keep going. If your reaction was unhealthy, do your best to describe it and then find a replacement behavior that you can live with.

Ask yourself if you have any habits that are holding you back. Do you have a short temper? A sharp tongue of sarcasm? A cold shoulder response when others hurt your feelings? A promiscuous lifestyle? An "I will hurt you before you hurt me" mindset? Briefly describe the habit:

Then pause and pray these words of a famous poet, King David:

> Search me, O God, and know my heart;
>   test me and know my anxious thoughts.
> See if there is any offensive way in me,
>   and lead me in the way everlasting.
>   (Psalm 139:23-24)

After praying this prayer, write down the insights the Holy Spirit brings to mind regarding this habit:

Now what is one step you can take to empty the emotional trash can of your life and become a healthier person?

Fit for Life: Physical Goodness

We are all inspired by guests on the TV show *The Biggest Loser,* such as Phil and Amy Parham, who lost a combined total of 256 pounds, then wrote hope for others in *The 90-Day Fitness Challenge*. At the same time, we are distressed when we encounter people who are needlessly out of shape and overweight. We don't want to overstate the issue because we know you have no choice over your body type, and many factors lead to weight and health problems. We just know that many opportunities are lost when people are out of shape.

We were recently enjoying a concert of talented singers and musicians when our hearts were moved for two reasons: 1) the music was performed to perfection, and 2) the artists were too young to be as out of shape as they appeared. I whispered to Bill, "This music is beautiful, but if the performers don't have a change of lifestyle, their lives will be cut short and the world will miss out on their talent." We don't expect these artists to become athletes, but we do long for their gifts to have a long shelf life.

Set Physical Goals

None of us improves our health by accident. We make progress because we develop a new view of ourselves through deliberate focus. What exercise goals do you have for this year? Do you want to start walking regularly, stay on track with your current program, or prepare for a competition? What are your weight goals for this year? Do you want to lose weight, gain weight, or maintain your weight?

Search Out Your Physical Aptitude

It is imperative that you explore your capacity to exert yourself physically. Some of us were made to run, while some were made to walk. Some of you reading this are wired for competition, and you love the intensity of athletic pursuits. Others of you think exercise is a form of medieval torture. The key is to find the way that you move best.

We were all made to move, but how we move is as varied as the cultures that decorate our world. So ask yourself, "What form of movement do I enjoy the most?" If you really don't like to move much, then ask, "What type of movement am I willing to put up with to protect my health?"

While watching the news recently, we heard that if you are overweight at 20, you will likely die eight years earlier than your peers.[6] To put it simply, it's worth it to keep moving.

Develop a Health Plan

It's wise to first consult your doctor to determine an effective plan for improving your health. He or she can create a baseline of your vital signs and blood work from which you can monitor your progress. Once you've consulted your doctor, you can supplement your plan with wellness experts dedicated to building healthy lives. One such resource is First Place 4 Health ministry.

First Place 4 Health is an international organization that has been helping people for 30 years. They offer Bible study groups and materials, workout videos, a supportive website with recipes, informational blogs, and more. They also offer a wellness week in various locations so people can spend focused time learning new lifestyle choices to live longer and stronger for God.

One of the most inspirational speakers on the team is Becky Turner, a single woman who lost and has kept off 46 pounds through First Place 4 Health. Her first good decision was to own up to the realization she had a problem. She needed to confess it, own it, and plan with God a way to get over it. Becky shares her thought process:

> Number one, there is nothing from which [God] cannot deliver me. Number two, He desired my cooperation in this process by pushing away from the table sooner, making wiser choices in my food and to exercise. Number three, food had become my idol and replaced Him.[7]

The most important part of the plan is your commitment to get what you need. We are adults and must take responsibility for the changes we want to experience. To be sure, parts of our lives only God can change, but He is interested in our full participation so that we grow to the potential of our maturity. I (Pam) want to have the longest run of influence I possibly can, so health and exercise are of special interest to me. I have, therefore, been compiling research on what each of us needs to become more healthy.

Get informed. Learn from professionals how to live healthily. Take classes, read books, subscribe to blogs, download audiobooks—even watch television shows featuring advice from doctors, nutritionists, fitness experts, and other health professionals.

Get moving. Get active and find exercise you enjoy. Hire a certified personal trainer if you haven't been active or want faster results. Your workout plan should be a balance between aerobics, strength training, core work, and balance enhancement.

Get drinking. By simply drinking 64 ounces of water a day, you can feel and look better.

Get your numbers. See your doctor for a comprehensive exam and get test results. You might also consider a more holistic medical expert. Some branches of medical science include natural foods, herbs, and supplements to augment health. (To find a physician with this specialty go to www.naturopathic.org.)

Get grazing. Small meals closer together will also keep your sugar level from spiking. Mini-snacks of 250 calories or less can keep your insulin levels down and lower your cholesterol.

Get shopping. Stock up on the right choices—increase your intake of fruits and vegetables while you lower the use of fried, sugared, and processed foods. Make your plate a rainbow of colors to increase your fruit and vegetable intake as recommended by the U.S. Department of Agriculture. You can create your own personalized food pyramid at www. mypyramid.gov.

Get tough. Arlene Pellicane, author of *31 Days to a Younger You*, recommends:

> Your first victory can happen right in the comfort and privacy of your own home, namely in your kitchen. You can do a very simple thing today to dramatically boost your health and drop a few pounds. Are you ready? Throw out the foods and drinks in your kitchen and pantry that stand in the way of optimum health and weight loss. What foods am I talking about? Cookies, chips, milk chocolate, candy bars, cake, soda, sugary drinks, TV dinners, white bread, bagels, and _____ (you fill in the blank).
>
> I said it was simple, not easy...
>
> The truth is, if you have easy access to something delicious and unhealthy, you will eat it...When your refrigerator is stocked with clean, cut fruits and vegetables, you will snack on those things. One battle for your body's health is won in the grocery store.[8]

Get friends. People with a supportive network make changes that stick. Join a walking club, a health club, a weight-loss group, a First Place 4 Health Bible study. If all your friends share the need to get in shape, challenge them to take this journey with you and go together to a health-club class or band together and form your own Bible study.

Get honest. When writing *The 10 Best Decisions a Woman Can Make*, I (Pam) discovered a startling fact that all of us can choose to implement in order to live longer. "The more friends you have, the healthier you are. However, this effect is due, almost exclusively, to the degree which you have talked with your friends about any traumas that you have suffered."[9]

Get motivated. Find that thing that propels you forward. I (Pam) reward myself for every major goal achieved by buying a new sports outfit or tool for fitness. (Girls, life is really about the outfits, right? And guys, life is better with cool gear, agreed?) When I started my midlife weight-reduction plan, I gave myself a new outfit every time I lost 10 pounds. Bill adds a Jacuzzi soak after a harsh strength-training circuit. I take a dip in the pool after an aerobic workout or a pedicure after a long morning hike. It can even be a small reward, such as giving myself permission to sit in the sun with a magazine or book. However, finding that sustainable motivation goes a little deeper. For example, when Bill or I look at a cookie, we ask, "Which do I want more, a cookie now or to be at my granddaughter's wedding 20 years from now?" The wedding wins every time!

Get shut-eye. By sleeping eight hours a night, you can actually lose weight. Wow, finally a diet plan we all love, "The sleep diet!"

Health expert Danna Demetre, author of *Scale Down*, says, "Small steps taken consistently will add up in big ways over time." Author Christin Ditchfield is a good example of how small steps make a big difference. She took Carole Lewis, the national director of First Place 4 Health, up on the challenge to *Give God a Year*.[10] Christin shares her journey of "small steps":

> A few years ago, I started having some serious health problems. In three years, I had eight major surgeries and at least twenty other "minor" medical conditions. After nearly two years of bed rest, my weight (which had always been a struggle) got completely out of control. My surgeries were ultimately unsuccessful, and last fall, I realized I will probably be living with chronic pain until Jesus comes back. I can't do anything about that. But what I can do is concentrate on alleviating or even eliminating the aches and pains that have come from post-op bed rest and inactivity. I can take better care of my overall health. I can choose to focus on all the things I have to be thankful for instead of focusing on the things I have lost. So that's what I've been doing. I've lost almost seventy pounds and got myself fit enough to walk a half-marathon![11]

Small steps do add up! So pause right now and ask God, *What small steps do You want me to begin to take:*

This week?

This month?

This year?

Work It Out: Vocational Goodness

When we did surveys and focus groups with singles, one thing rang loud and clear. When it comes to income, singles grasp the harsh reality, "We are on our own!" It is vital, therefore, that you commit to a career path that offers adequate compensation. God made us to work, and we all have a stronger sense of well-being when we have a career we enjoy and one that provides for our financial needs.

Set Career Goals

Psalm 37:4 says, "Delight yourself in the LORD and he will give you the desires of your heart." Proverbs 16:9 gives marching orders for our goals, "In his heart a man plans his course, but the LORD determines his steps." We plan the course, but God directs our steps. Be bold, therefore, and set goals for what you want to accomplish in your career. Say to Jesus,

- This year, I want to accomplish the following in my career...
- I want to reach the following position in my career...
- I want to be known for...

Search Out Your Career Aptitude

Your career capacity begins with your natural talents, but it is not limited to those talents. As you explore your career path, first take into account the abilities that are a natural part of the way you have been made. Then add in the God factor. I (Pam) am known for saying to our audiences, "Show me the size of your God, and I will show you the size of your opportunity. Show me the size of your God, and I'll show you the size of your adventure. Big God, big opportunity. Big God, big adventure." In *Woman of Confidence*, I include advice from wise leaders and mentors that shows how to grow God-sized confidence:

- "The truth is self-confident people aren't necessarily brimming with talent, skill, or physical beauty; they just feel they are. They think differently than their less assured peers."—Dr. Mark Goulston

- "What comes into our minds when we think about God is the most important thing about us."—A.W. Tozer, *The Knowledge of the Holy*

- "How I live my life is a testimony of what I believe about God."—Henry Blackaby and Claude King, *Experiencing God*

- "Who we believe God is greatly affects our eternal destinies, but I'd like to suggest that nothing has a greater effect on the quality of our lives and the fulfillment of our destinies…we're wise to ask ourselves the question, Who do I say God is?"—Beth Moore

See the pattern? The more accurately we comprehend God, the bigger our faith becomes. As your faith grows, God can entrust you with more opportunities, dreams, and adventures. When we believe God is all He claims to be, we can draw on His resources to empower us. Second Corinthians 3:5 (NASB) says it like this, "Not that we are adequate in ourselves to consider anything as coming from ourselves, but our adequacy is from God."

When we tap into who God is—all-knowing, all-mighty, wise, true, faithful (the list of His names and traits goes on and on)—we find the strength to believe God for big things, good things, for our careers, our lives, and the world around us.

So pause right now and pray, "God, help me dream God-sized dreams for my career. You know it is just You and me, God, so show me the plan and path of success. In John 10:10, Jesus, You said You came that we might have life abundantly. Show me those plans, show me that life. I am listening. I am surrendered to Your will for me because I know You love me and have my best interests, and the best interests of all those You created, on Your heart. Amen."

Write down some God-sized dreams for your career:

Develop a Plan

What is the first step in getting there? Do you need more education, specialized training, boldness to talk with a boss or supervisor, courage to launch out on your own, wisdom from a mentor who has succeeded in this path and plan, funds to step out and be a business owner or to get that degree? Do you need a new skill, such as technology training, sales techniques, or social networking savvy? Write down three specific steps you can take this year that can become resources for God to use to move you forward:

1.

2.

3.

We Are Family: Relational Goodness

When songs become hits, it's often because something in them echoes and resonates in the hearts of the masses. "We Are Family," a late-seventies dance tune sung by Sister Sledge, is a classic song utilized throughout the past three decades to promote the interconnectedness of people who care about each other. This song has been popular because we all recognize that we need a family. Nearly every single we surveyed in preparation for this book mentioned the need to create a network of relationships that acted as a family.

Sometimes the network is necessary for practical reasons. If you don't have a spouse, you may need to recruit help when it's time to move, paint a room, or fix a leaky faucet. You need supportive friends when your car quits and you need that last-minute ride to work or church. Many things in life cannot be done alone, and if you are single, you need people you can call who won't hesitate to help.

Sometimes the network is for recreational or social reasons. Who do you share victories at work with or celebrate birthdays with? Who will be your support team when you go on that missions trip or encourage you as you launch that new business idea?

One single said it plainly, "As a single I have to embrace the fact I am not an island. I do need people. But I can select those I call 'family.' My advice: Know who you will call in an emergency, be careful in selecting who gets the keys to your place to watch it while you travel or to care for pets, be picky in deciding who will surround your life."

Another single chimed in, "Friendship is enjoyable—but also a necessity!"

Remember Becky Turner, who lost all that weight? What was the real secret to her success? Becky confessed her mistakes, but then she made a smart plan toward victory. And the key to winning the battle of the bulge? Friends.

> First, there was Carole—a wiser, older woman who had lived this lifestyle of health for many years. She was giving her adult children the greatest gift she could give them—her good health. We would meet as often as possible—usually each weekday—to exercise, quote memory verses and always close out our time together in prayer.
>
> Another godly friend was Vicki. God used her in my life to help me remember who I was not. I was no longer a fuzzy, ground-crawling caterpillar, but I was transformed into a beautiful monarch butterfly! She did this in many different ways, but one of the greatest ways was by helping me shop and pick out clothes. That's what girlfriends do, right?

Another lifelong friend God brought into my life was Karrie. Those that know me know how strong-willed and stubborn I was, and I needed a full-time "Nathan" in my life. Nathans are those people in your life who point out sin and weakness but then walk along beside you to help you to make it right. Even though Karrie lives hundreds of miles away from me, I'd fax my food diary to her. She's the one who contacts me and asks me if I exercised that day.

In my pride, I wish I could do it all on my own, but it really does take a community. I thank God for the First Place community. It makes deliverance, freedom and abundant living not just a theological concept but a day in and day out reality. I am still a work in progress, but I am not where I used to be. And through God's grace and the gift of accountability, I will never go back to that place again.[12]

Many singles live far from family or come from broken or dysfunctional families. Their friendship circle becomes a kind of family that shares holiday meals, celebrates successes, and supports each other when a trauma happens. The key to having a strong team around you when you need it is to invest in relationships ahead of time. Cultivate friendships with like-minded people who share your values. Create your own "small group" where you can share authentically, and as the Bible encourages, "carry each other's burdens" (Galatians 6:2).

The healthiest singles we know proactively build traditions into their lives to cultivate their relationships. One hosts a yearly New Year's Eve dinner party. Another hosts a "Night at the Oscars" dress-up dinner during the Academy Awards. They watch the broadcast to see the winners, but they feel like winners themselves as they celebrate their friendship dressed to the nines. One of our male friends cultivates his friendships around major sporting events: Super Bowl, World Cup soccer, Wimbledon, the Final Four, and the World Series. One of the singles in our family has sometimes lived too far away to take part in family gatherings at Thanksgiving and Christmas. On those years, she serves in a local soup kitchen, hands out gifts for Angel Tree prison ministry, and hosts her friends for an evening of good food, great laughs, and greater memories. One Irish friend uses St Patrick's Day as his holiday of choice to gather his friends and family.

Think about your needs. Do you know the three or four people you'd call if the world turned upside down on you today? Thank those friends for being there for you, and extend the umbrella by inviting others to join your circle of friends. Do you have a friend you trust to talk with about your finances, your home, your love life, your career, your car?

Brain Check: Intellectual Goodness

It's easy to get into an intellectual rut. We feel good when we are the expert in an area; we feel stupid in social circles where we lack wisdom and knowledge. In addition, those who *use* their minds are less likely to *lose* their minds. So keep stimulated intellectually. We experience growth every time we learn something new. The people we talk to, the books (and blogs) we read, the movies and TV programs we watch, along with the new vistas we experience make us stronger and more interesting. Expand your horizons. Set goals to go new places, read new things, meet new people, and learn new skills.

Set Intellectual Growth Goals

Set intellectual growth goals by completing these sentences:

> Someone I would love to have coffee with is…
>
> A place in the world I would love to travel to is…
>
> A new skill I'd love to acquire is…
>
> A new book or a new author I'd like to read is…
>
> A new movie, stage drama, Broadway play I'd like to see is…
>
> A new subject I'd like to know how to talk about is…
>
> The people group or generation of people I'd like to know more about is…

Determine Your Intellectual Aptitude

You will be enthusiastic about the information you care about, so your aptitude begins with the question, "What topics do you find most interesting?" In addition, each of us has a limit of how many words and experiences we can absorb at a time. Some of you have an enormous capacity, so you can read and write all the time. We all know people who fill their Facebook, Twitter, and email with constant interaction and interesting facts. Others of you do well if you learn one new thought per day. Wherever you fall on the spectrum, thank God for the capacity you have and live it out every day.

Develop an Intellectual Growth Plan

Sign up for a class, recruit someone to mentor you, buy the ticket to travel. Make that call to a person you can walk with, dine with, or have coffee with to bridge a gender gap, a cultural gap, or a generational gap. Create a "do something new" or "meet someone new" reminder in your computer or phone calendar that will appear once a week or once a month.

Upward Reach: Spiritual Goodness

No one loves you and values you more than Jesus. If a brave, selfless person stepped in front of an assassin's scope and "took the bullet" in your place, wouldn't you want to know him? That is a picture of what Jesus did. He is like your personal secret service agent who volunteered for the job of caring for you. Don't you want a deep, authentic relationship with someone who is that devoted to you and authentic in His love for you? If so, tell Jesus you want to know Him—then dig in and get to know Him.

Set Spiritual Goals

If we want to grow in any relationship, we have to spend time with the other person. In the same way, if we want to grow with God, we need to spend time with Him, hear the words on His heart, and apply His wisdom to our lives. Cultivating a daily personal time with Christ is an essential component of your spiritual growth.

Search Out Your Aptitude

Pam and I discovered early on that we have different spiritual paces. I like it best when I can spend one to two hours at a time in study and prayer. I can't do this every day, so each day I spend a few minutes reading my Bible and praying, and then I make an appointment with Jesus once a week to study for a longer period. Pam prefers a consistent 15 minutes every day. As soon as she discovers an application from the Bible, she gets motivated to start doing it, so it works best for her to spread out the learning daily.

Learn what works best for you, and then make sure you schedule that time on your calendar.

Develop a Spiritual Growth Plan

The heart of your growth is the time you spend with your Savior. Here are some ways to enhance your personal time with Him:

1. *Pick a place.* Where is the best location to have some undivided quiet time to read the Bible, do a Bible study, listen to the Bible on audio? Where do you have the most privacy—in your home, your car, or your office?

2. *Pick a time.* What time of day can you be most consistent? For many, early morning provides the least distractions. For others, winding down at the end of the day helps them sleep peacefully. Others find sitting at their desk before the workday gives the most consistent rhythm to life. Be realistic on the length of time each day. It is better to set a goal of 5-10 minutes and do it *every day* than to do one day for 90 minutes, then miss for the next nine days.

3. *Pick a method.* Here are some ideas to help you dig more out of the Bible:

A, E, I, O, U

A—*Ask questions.* See if you can come up with 10 questions to ask of the text.

E—*Emphasize.* Find definitions for key words and phrases. (You'll need a dictionary, a Bible dictionary, and maybe a Bible encyclopedia.)

I—*In your own words.* Paraphrase the verse or a portion of the passage you're studying.

O—Other references. If your Bible has cross-references, use those to lead you to other passages that discuss the same topic.

U—You! Choose a personal application. The sooner you can apply it, the better.

Question It

Print out entire sections of Scripture in double-space format, and then begin to mark it up and ask questions to guide your study of this passage. You can find a variety of Bible translations online at BibleGateway. com. Ask:

- *Who*: Who wrote it and to whom?
- *What*: What is the context of this story? What is going on before and after this passage?
- *When*: When did it take place in history? Are there some things I need to know about the culture?
- *Where*: Can I find it on a map?
- *Why*: What was the writer's motivation? Is this a teaching passage? A poem that shares feeling? A story that illustrates a point?
- *How*: How does this apply to life today? To my life?

1, 2, 3

I (Pam) learned three simple questions as an 18-year-old college student that launched me into the Bible daily:

- *What does it say*? (What are the facts? What's going on in the passage?)
- *What does it mean?* (Do I understand the meaning, or do I need to investigate some word by looking up its meaning? Do I need to cross reference some other verses to see where else this is talked about in the Bible? Do I need to investigate culture, history, or commentators' views to understand what this passage meant to its original readers?)

- *What does it mean to me?* (How can I apply it today to my life?)

There are many other more complex Bible study methods, and if you want to consistently dig deeper, we suggest *Living by the Book* by Howard Hendricks and William Hendricks; *How to Read the Bible for All Its Worth* by Gordon Fee and Douglas Stuart; *The New How to Study Your Bible* by Kay Arthur, David Arthur, and Pete DeLacy; or the GodSquad website (www.godsquad.com/discipleship/inductive.htm).

Pick a Layer

For the busy person, layering God's Word through your life will enhance your spiritual growth. Put the Bible on your smartphone, on your iPod, or carry the Bible on CDs in your car. You can also post verses as your screensaver, computer password, or on memory cards that you carry with you or tape to your bathroom mirror. Decorate your home with fine art that includes a verse or decorate your refrigerator door with Scripture. Place quiet-time baskets in every room of your home with a different version of the Bible, a journal, and a devotional by some of your favorite authors. If you get a few minutes in that room, you can choose to spend some extra time with God. Enroll in blogs, email devotionals, and blog feeds from ministries that will send a devotional to your inbox once a week or once a day. Tune your satellite radio to the Christian stations and preset your car stereo to stations that feature Christian preaching and teaching.

What can you do to deepen your walk with God:

This week?

This month?

This year?

Outward Focus: Inspirational Goodness

As we interviewed singles for this book, it became obvious that those who were the happiest were deeply involved in the lives of others. They were serving at their churches, volunteering for nonprofits, working in their communities, and traveling for missions or humanitarian work. They found their fulfillment in encouraging missionaries, helping with a project to benefit others, or using their talents to address a significant need in the world around them.

Having an outward focus can feel overwhelming when you consider all the needs in the world, but every person can meet at least one need. So where do you begin in your journey toward altruism? Congratulations, you already have! By picking up this book and learning about your passion, your uniqueness, your calling, and your skill set, you have embarked on the journey of discovering the best you can offer back to Jesus. Your calling is simply where the world's need meets your passion. So let's identify the areas you might serve and reach most effectively:

Under each item below, check which option you most prefer:

1. I prefer to spend time helping:

   ☐ Those younger than me

   ☐ Those older than me

   ☐ My peers

2. I prefer helping through:

   ☐ One-on-one interactions

   ☐ Small group settings

   ☐ Involvement with a larger team

   ☐ Being in charge of a larger team

3. I enjoy being:

   ☐ Mostly outdoors

   ☐ Mostly indoors

4. I prefer this kind of setting:

☐ I am flexible and roughing it seems exciting, and I like a new adventure in hard to reach places.

☐ Basic needs like a hot shower, indoor plumbing, and hot food make me less grumpy and more effective.

☐ I am flexible, but I do like a few comforts of home.

☐ I enjoy staying in a host home or in economy lodging that keeps me in touch with locals, but has some amenities I am used to.

☐ I need a soft bed and nice surroundings to be my best. Yeah, I know I might be a little higher maintenance, but I still love others!

5. I enjoy giving time:

☐ A few hours every week

☐ A day once a week

☐ A few days once a month

☐ About a week or more once a year

Now look at the answers you gave. This should help you see the setting to best place yourself, your gifts, and your passion. Nothing is set in stone, so you can always try various options, but this gives you a good starting point—or restarting point—for how, when, and where to be more other-focused.

You Decide

It takes focused effort, but you will enjoy your life more when you commit to live a good life. So set some goals, search out your aptitude, and design a plan, and then watch what God can do.

Just for Fun

A lot of times worrying about life keeps us up at night. Did you hear about the dyslexic agonstic insomniac? He lay awake at night wondering if there really was a dog.

CHAPTER 8

Decide to Be an Influencer

"The fruit of the Spirit is...faithfulness."

GALATIANS 5:22

You have been given a life of influence and it revolves around your story. No one in history has exactly the same story you have. God has been building your story in concert with His sovereign plan. He has allowed you to go through a number of experiences because He is grooming you for the people you are supposed to influence.

Think about it. Many things have happened in your life that you didn't deserve. Some of these experiences are positive blessings you have received that you are sure you didn't earn. Life has just been kind to you in some areas. Other areas are negative experiences that are likewise undeserved. You didn't do enough wrong to warrant the treatment you received, but it happened anyway. If you are a thinking person, you have asked, "Why has this stuff happened in my life?"

Well, the primary reason is that God allowed you to have these experiences so that others could be helped by them. The undeserved blessings you have been given provide you with opportunities to lead, teach, and inspire others. The good things that have happened in your life remind others that God is in the habit of doing good things for them too. When you talk about the progress you have made, it inspires others to believe they can make progress also.

The negative experiences you have struggled through are examples of how God redeems. We all live day by day "while we wait for the blessed hope—the glorious appearing of our great God and Savior, Jesus Christ, who gave himself for us to redeem us from all wickedness and to purify for himself a people that are his very own, eager to do what is good" (Titus 2:13-14).

Since we live in a world that is infected by evil, it is common for each of us to suffer hardship, pain, and significant disappointments. It is almost unbelievable how many ways humans can abuse and take advantage of others. Parents hurt their children. Friends manipulate even their best friends. Business partners betray one another. Leaders exploit their followers, and followers subvert their leaders' plans.

Then there's the whole world of guy/gal relationships. People who start out being romantically interested in one another end up being angry, manipulative, petty, and jealous. And sometimes, those who appeared to be romantic interests weren't interests at all. They were simply prowlers looking for victims.

In a world like this, we need loads of people who are willing to let the experience of their pain and redemption be an example for others. We need people who are willing to talk about their hurts without being pathetic, and who can share how God helped them overcome the pain as they discovered a new way to live filled with forgiveness and deliberate skill development.

The good news is that you don't have to take extreme measures to have influence in the lives of others. You just need to embrace your story. Be faithful in telling your story and living out a life God can use as an example of hope and help. Your story includes how you came to faith, the influence of your family, and the most significant points of growth in your life. Pam recently posted this on her Facebook page:

> Revelation 12:11: "They overcame him by the blood of the Lamb and by the word of their testimony." Power in Jesus' death on the cross for us + Power of telling our story = people overcome and finding new life, new hope.

As you become more in touch with your story, the future path of your life becomes clearer, and the decisions you need to make to get there become more focused.

Your story is unique to you. We all have certain traits in common, but only you have your unique combination of traits, experiences, and significant moments. Let us share a few stories from the Bible that illustrate this point. The first two stories portray influential men in the New Testament who have very different stories.

Paul's Mission Impossible

First, let's take a look at the apostle Paul. He recounts his story in Galatians 1:13-24. He was raised in a devout Jewish home and had a passion for the Hebrew ways. He was more committed than his peers and was advancing faster and farther than others his age. His youthful enthusiasm turned into extreme zeal to the point that he persecuted the church and tried to destroy it. He ignorantly thought he was serving God when in reality he had become God's enemy.

God's grace was bigger than Paul's zeal, however, and Jesus interrupted Paul's life on the road to Damascus and called him to preach to the Gentiles. Paul was the most devout Jew of his day, and God called him to be an evangelist to the Gentiles so that all could see in living color how powerful God's grace is.

Paul's transformation created instant humility in this strong leader. He knew he had to start over. His religious zeal was so intense that he knew he couldn't just drop one life to start living another. He needed training and plenty of it. After his supernatural encounter with Jesus, he went to Arabia and Damascus for three years so he could get schooled in his newfound faith and purpose. After three years of discipleship, he went to Jerusalem to connect with Peter and James and to be introduced to the community of believers.

You can imagine what a scandal this could have been. Paul was well known as the fiercest enemy of the newly born church of Jesus. He had a track record of arresting believers and putting them to death. He could not just show up and announce that he was now part of the church. People would never believe him unless he was confidently endorsed by the right people. He, therefore, had to gain the confidence of Peter, who was the leader among the apostles, and James, the brother of Jesus, who was a prominent leader of the church in Jerusalem.

Eventually, Paul was fully integrated into the community of believers and became the most prolific church planter of his day and the author of approximately half the New Testament. He is certainly an example to all of us of hard work, dedication, and persistence. More importantly, he is proof that no one is too far gone or too hostile to be captured by God's grace. God can take anyone with any life story and transform that person into a highly effective servant. God is faithful.

Timothy's Steady Pace

Timothy's story is far different from Paul's. His is a story of steady growth amidst struggles. We learn the highlights of his story in 2 Timothy 1:3-7. He was a sensitive man who was not ashamed to cry when it was appropriate. He was also gifted when it came to friendships. People did better when they were around him. They had greater confidence, were more joyful, and created long-lasting memories when they spent time with him.

He grew up in a solid, believing family. His mother and grandmother had a strong, sincere faith, which he caught and adopted in his own life. We don't know why his dad is not mentioned, but it is clear that the women in his life had a profound impact on his development.

He had a significant spiritual experience that confirmed his calling as a pastor and bestowed on him a specific gift for ministry (1 Timothy 4:14; 2 Timothy 1:6). It appears that Timothy was either naturally content or a little overwhelmed by the calling, because he needs encouragement to maximize its influence. Rather than do all he can to develop this gift, he needs to be challenged by his friends and held accountable. He gets moving when he is told to fan the flame and to rely on the power and love of the Spirit.

Timothy is a great example for everyone who grew up in a stable, believing home. Timothy's story is neither spectacular nor stunning. There is no great transformation where he changed from an enemy of God to a fervent servant. He grows at a slow but steady pace. He does what is right because it is right, and he calmly makes commitments to help people. Even though he doesn't have a dramatic story to tell, he was one the most influential leaders of the first-century church. He was entrusted with significant responsibility, and he was trusted as a solid teacher.

Just as these men's stories have inspired people throughout history, your story counts also. We all tend to think that only important people have stories worth telling, but the truth is that God is working in everyone, including you, to move His plan forward.

Two of the most quoted sayings of Jesus involve women who remain anonymous, and one of them didn't even know she was part of the story. In John 8, we find Jesus setting up shop in the temple on a very ordinary day. After he had gathered a crowd and began to teach, the Pharisees brought to him a woman caught in adultery. That is all we know about her. We aren't told whether she got involved in an adulterous relationship because she was rich and bored or because she was lonely and needy. We don't know if she was single or married or had children. We only know she was caught in adultery.

There is nothing remarkable about her except that the religious leaders brought her to Jesus in an attempt to test His commitment to the Law of Moses. We also have no idea what she did after her encounter with the Savior. We don't know if she continued to live immorally or if she embraced Jesus' challenge to live righteously. What we do know is that her story was the backdrop for one of the most profound statements Jesus made during his earthly ministry: "If any one of you is without sin, let him be the first to throw a stone at her" (John 8:7).

Then there's the widow who humbly showed up at the temple to give her offering. She was not well known by the crowd, and she had very little to contribute. She didn't announce her offering because it was so small; it wouldn't realistically meet any need. She obviously didn't make much of an income, she was never consulted on decisions, and nobody sought out her influence. And yet her actions formed the foundation for Jesus' teaching on voluntary giving: "This poor widow has put in more than all the others. All these people gave their gifts out of their wealth; but she out of her poverty put in all she had to live on" (Luke 21:3-4). Jesus wanted His disciples to realize that true giving comes from the heart and always involves a sacrifice. If there is no sacrifice, there is no movement of the heart. This woman demonstrated without a doubt that her love for God was the most important thing in her life.

Perhaps the most remarkable thing about her story is she didn't know she was helping Jesus communicate one of His most important lessons. There is no account that Jesus talked to her. There is no account of any face-to-face encounter before or after this event. There is no record that anyone ever told her what Jesus said about her gift. She most likely continued her very ordinary, difficult existence with no idea that her life counted for anything. We are sure she knows now how significant her life was, but she had no idea at the time.

To say that your story matters does not mean that people are interested in every little detail of your journey. People are not inspired by rambling stories that begin, "I was born at a very young age..." What people want to know about your story are the significant moments and experiences that inspire them to be better people.

Telling Your Story

How You Got to Be Who You Are Today

Your story begins with the family you grew up in. Your family had a number of traits, both positive and negative. Some of these traits created an intense response in you that helped you become who you are today. In addition, you've made decisions that added to the development of your character, preferences, and life skills. People are interested in hearing about these.

To help identify the influence your family had on you, fill in the chart below. In the first column, describe your family. These traits may be of your family as a whole (we are loving, affectionate, hard-working, react emotionally to things, never say, "I'm sorry") or they may be descriptions of individual family members (Dad was demanding, Dad was very loyal, Mom gave great advice, Mom was overly sensitive, my sister was manipulative). Don't worry about how many traits you have on the list. It doesn't have to include everything you know about your family because you didn't respond to everything your family did. You are looking for the traits that rise to the surface when you give yourself permission to think about them.

In the second column, do your best to describe your response to each of these traits. Most likely you have either adopted the same trait or you have reacted against it. For instance, if you grew up in an affectionate family, you are either affectionate yourself or you are very independent out of a strong sense of security. If your mother or father was demanding, you are either demanding yourself or you have a high sense of compassion for the shortcomings of others.

Don't overanalyze your life as you engage in this exercise. This is not designed to be a heavy therapy session; it's intended simply to help you recognize the influence your family has had on who you are today.

Traits of My Family	My Response	Keep	Replace
		☐	☐
		☐	☐
		☐	☐
		☐	☐
		☐	☐
		☐	☐
		☐	☐
		☐	☐
		☐	☐
		☐	☐

Once you've identified the influences of your family, choose whether you want to keep or replace them. For each trait, check the appropriate box. For the ones you want to keep, thank God for them and let them be a significant part of your story. Since you learned these in your most formative years from the most influential people in your life, they are easy to implement. You'll want to rely on these learned skills and put them into action as often as possible.

The traits you want to change take more work. You have probably made changes already in some of these areas. You may or may not have had a deliberate plan for making these changes, but you experienced enough discomfort that you knew change was necessary. Don't be hesitant to share these victories as part of your story. Everyone grew up in an imperfect family and has changes to make. The story of your progress can provide clarity and motivation to others.

Some traits require much more focused effort and a deliberate choice to change. The process is much easier to describe than to implement because these traits are deeply embedded. It takes a bit of desperation to change them. You have to be weary of the way your life is being affected and highly motivated to change. If you are at that point with a trait on your list, here are some recommendations for how to effect that change.

First, *describe the response you are not satisfied with*. Don't overanalyze this. It shouldn't take hours of study to figure this out. To be sure, there are stubborn areas of development that require the help of a trained counselor or spiritual leader, but we can bring about most changes with the current skills we possess. You can't change what you can't describe, however, so you must be able to reasonably describe your current responses if you are going to change any of them. You don't need to know every detail about the way you react. You just need a working knowledge of what sets you off and the unhealthy or unproductive way you respond.

Second, once you've described your natural response, describe *the new way you want to respond to the messages you receive*. This will take a deliberate decision and diligent practice. You'll have to practice the new response over and over until it becomes a habit. It has been estimated that a new habit takes 21 consecutive days to develop. This is not a universal rule but an indication that a new way of life takes focused, patient effort. You developed the current response by practicing it over and over until it established itself as a pattern. In the same way, you can practice a different response until it becomes second nature.

These then become the decisions you've made that help make you who you are. You are not a victim who has no choice but to live out what you were taught as a child. You have the ability to choose. You can stay the way you are, change a little, or change dramatically. You have no choice over what you started your journey with, but you have a lot of choice over what you end your journey with. God is faithful to implement change but you must be willing to want it.

The Significant Spiritual Moments in Your Life

The vital moments of your spiritual journey form the second part of your story that people want to hear. A walk with Jesus is a marathon, and many of the moments along the way are not really worth recounting. There a few moments, however, that become the signature of what God is doing in our lives. These moments inspire others and remind them of God's interest in us.

Moses was 80 years into his journey when he encountered the burning bush. Joshua was about 80 years old when he led the charge on Jericho. Rahab was instrumental in the success of the Israeli spies, but we hear nothing about her life prior to this event. We don't want to hear all the details. We're not interested in the daily process of shepherding that occupied most of Moses' adult life. We don't really care what day 3000 was like in the wilderness of Sinai for Joshua. It does not inspire us to hear about Rahab's daily chores. There are moments, however, in each of these lives that challenge us to be stronger and remind us of God's faithfulness.

Your life is the same way. Nobody wants to hear all the details, but there are moments that demonstrate God's interest in you and the possibilities that exist through a partnership with Jesus. I (Bill) would never expect you to endure an explanation of all the days I've spent studying. I would also never attempt to describe the nuances of my prayer life. I do get excited, however, to share with you a few of the most significant moments in my spiritual growth.

Without a doubt, the most significant day in my life was the day I went to see the movie, *The Exorcist.* I was 16 years old and full of adolescent confidence. I'd had very little exposure to church and had never read any part of the Bible. When I watched this movie, I came face-to-face with a spiritual reality I knew nothing about. I knew Hollywood had overdone it, but I had heard the story was based on something true, and I couldn't see anything different between the girl on the screen and me. I left asking myself, *If that could happen to her, what would stop it from happening to me?*

I left with no answers and began reading a Bible that sat undisturbed in our home to see if I could find any help there. After a month of sleepless nights and consistent reading, I read 1 John 4:4, "the one who is in you is greater than the one who is in the world." This verse opened my eyes and heart to my need to know Jesus. The night I asked Christ to be my Savior was a day that changed my life. Peace entered my heart so that

I began to sleep again, and a relentless motivation to figure out what Jesus was about was born in my soul.

I now live with a conviction that Jesus knows how to find His people. I wasn't looking for Him. I wasn't reading books about spiritual things or searching for truth. I wasn't feeling lonely, lost, or lousy about my life. I just went to a movie—but Jesus knew He could find me there.

Another significant moment in my spiritual growth took place when my kids were young. I was visiting my parents when my mom did something that made me madder than I can ever remember being. My mom has been a strong influence throughout my life. Her creativity and energy have inspired me, but the major impact has been negative. She was afraid of most things and had an irrational need to be in charge. She was often angry and would lecture for hours. She was critical, demanding, and often just didn't make sense as she let fear run her life.

I had been pretty good at ignoring her until I became a dad. I don't even remember what she did that day, but I am still very aware of my reaction. I put my kids in the car and left immediately. I gripped the steering wheel so hard my knuckles were literally white. I'm surprised I didn't break the steering wheel. It took me two hours to relax my grip and start talking in normal tones.

Prior to this event, I had read about forgiveness and even taught on forgiveness, but I wasn't really committed to live a life of forgiveness. As I was steaming over my mom, the Holy Spirit was whispering to me, "This is how you will be if you don't forgive. If you want your mom to have this kind of influence in your life, just choose to ignore her rather than forgive her. If you want to be free from this anger, however, you have to forgive her the same way I forgave you."

It stunned me. I knew in an instant that I needed to figure this out. The process of forgiveness didn't become clear all at once, but the motivation to get there was ignited in a way that would never be extinguished.

Sometimes we withhold forgiveness because we think, *That person doesn't deserve forgiveness.* You are correct, none of us deserve forgiveness; because we are all sinners, we all deserve hell. But God in His mercy forgave us. Our friend Dorothy Ross penned a few lines that aptly describe why we should forgive: "I forgave to set a prisoner free, then I came to realize the prisoner had been me."

I've been walking with Jesus for over 30 years, and yet I can demonstrate Christ's impact on my life in a few short stories. In the space below, briefly note the most significant spiritual experiences of your life. These markers might help you recall some of the moments God has been faithful to you:

What brought you into a relationship with God?

What are some of the decisions of obeying God that have made your life better, richer, fuller, more satisfying?

How has God used your life to make the world a better place or to help another?

Have there been significant moments that helped you figure out yourself or life better?

Other magnificent moments of God's faithfulness:

Moments of Clarity

In addition to the spiritual moments that have propelled you forward, there are moments when certain life skills came into focus or answers to questions finally arrived. These moments take years to set up as you synchronize your interest, maturity level, information, and willingness to grow. When these all come together, breakthroughs happen. Thoughts that used to be confusing become clear. Skills that used to be awkward become smooth. Issues that used to knock you off balance lose their effect on you. Since everyone faces situations that are frustrating, confusing, and disappointing, the things you have figured out are helpful to others.

The Nuggets of Insight You Have That Can Help Others

In some areas of life, you've been able to boil down important tasks, attitudes, and thoughts into simple statements or procedures. These nuggets of insight result in simple processes or statements that you do and say consistently. Each time you share it, somebody's life is affected positively. Some of the simple statements that have helped me (Bill) are:

"Where there is light, there are bugs."

I heard this at a chapel service while I was attending Talbot Seminary in Southern California. I was frustrated that churches were hard to run and that being a pastor was such a strenuous pursuit. This statement reset my perspective. I realized when I heard it that difficulties are normal when people gather together for any significant purpose. Problems in church were not an interruption; they were evidence that good things were happening.

"Experience is what you get when you don't get what you want."

I read this on a bumper sticker one day, and it became the moment I realized that God never wastes an opportunity. The good times in life encourage us, but the tough times give us maturity, persistence, and increased capacity.

"Do the big things first."

I once heard someone speak on the importance of priorities, and the speaker pulled out a box of rocks and sand and a large glass jar. He placed the biggest rocks in the jar first followed by smaller rocks and finally filled in with sand. His point was if you start with the sand, there will not be room for the rocks at the end. If, however, you put the biggest rocks in first, there will be room for all the smaller items.

Priorities began to make sense to me that day. Prior to that, I would have told you priorities were important, but what I learned that day has caused me to ask, *What are the most important things I need to do today? Let's do those first!*

"Dreams are free."

I don't even remember when this statement became part of my vocabulary, but I find I quote it often. During my thirties, I began to realize that life is a bigger struggle than I had thought. Disappointments, frustrated plans, and mistakes can drain the life out of our dreams. I began to realize that most people lose their creativity to avoid more disappointments. They settle into a routine life with few surprises and shallow hopes. Somewhere along the way, I realized that it costs nothing to dream about having a bigger life. Although most dreams don't come true, the commitment to dream adds creativity and fosters a sense of anticipation.

"The Bible was written in common language."

God led the writers of the New Testament to use Koine Greek, the language that common workers and average citizens would understand. When I first heard this, my view of what it meant to study the Bible changed. It was no longer an intellectual pursuit trying to be smart about God's Word. It became an attempt to bridge two cultures. I realized that if I had lived in the New Testament era, the Bible would have been clear to me. It would have been written in my language and would have used illustrations from a culture I was familiar with. We live in a day and culture that is different. Studying helps us bridge that gap. This conclusion unleashed the simple power of the Bible. Rather than looking for the deep stuff, I began to focus on the obvious stuff.

"Do the obvious."

My mentor said this to me as an offhanded comment after I had asked his advice about something. I don't remember what the issue was, but I have never forgotten that God usually makes the next thing in life obvious. Rather than waste time trying to figure out the things in the fog, plenty of progress can be made by simply doing what obviously needs to be done.

Some of my (Pam's) favorite nuggets of insight are:

"Sometimes the dots don't connect."

This was said to me at a difficult time in our life when people and circumstances didn't make sense to me. It freed me from trying to figure out why or how come. Instead of trying to figure out people or circumstances,

I set my face to achieve the goals already on my calendar and agenda. Often we allow other people's drama to knock us off stride when it is in our best interests just to work the plan He gave. It isn't necessary to understand other people's drama and chaos to follow God's plan for our lives. I still cannot explain why some of the circumstances I thought were so unfair and hurtful happened, but I do know God faithfully walked us through. Someday in heaven it will all make sense. All I know is that by sticking to the call God had already given to me to do, lots of people were helped even when I couldn't make sense of all the swirling circumstances around me.

"Do the next thing."

Elisabeth Elliot, wife of slain missionary Jim Elliot, is known for saying this, and it has been a token of great wisdom. When I don't know the big plan, I just do the next right thing. Too often people place life on hold waiting for "God to speak." But God often leads step by step first before He gives the big picture, giving light for only the next step on the path. My friend Jane Rubietta puts it like this, "God is working just beyond the headlights of your life." Knowing God is working for me makes things okay, even if I cannot see Him work. All He wants is for me to faithfully accomplish the next right thing or take care of the next person. In doing so, God will ensure I arrive at the big picture or gain the overall vision for my life.

"Those who honor God, He will honor."

This is a simple phrase from 1 Samuel 2:30 that we raised our sons with and that they have memorized.

"Be ALIVE."

Our friend Ken Nichols is known for this phrase, which forms a simple acrostic:

Always

Live

In

View of

Eternity

And every decision is easier for Ken with this as the backdrop of his heart.

You, likewise, have things to share that have become basic to you. Do you have some bumper sticker, catchphrase, or coffee mug slogan that helps you move your life forward? They may be sayings that bring clarity. They may be processes that you can explain easily. They may be problem-solving skills that simplify decisions for others. The key is that God has entrusted this nugget to you so that you can help others. If you keep it to yourself, it loses its impact. If you share it often, many people will benefit from the treasure God has placed in you.

Write down some phrases here that can become a part of your story of God's faithfulness in your life. As you unfold your story, these simple phrases will help your message stick with people. Make note of the sayings you use most often, the tasks that are simple for you, and the insights you have that others often ask for.

Questions to Discover Your Uniqueness

A question believers commonly ask is, "How can I know the will of God for my life?" Each of us has a sense that we are on this earth for some purpose, but we spend much of our time wondering how we can figure out what that purpose is. Fortunately, God wants us to know His will even more than we want to know it. He Himself said,

> I will instruct you and teach you in the way
>   which you should go;
> I will counsel you with My eye upon you.
>   (Psalm 32:8 NASB)

Life is decorated with many choices, but those choices also complicate the decision-making landscape. The more options you have and the more talented you are, the more people will want from you. You need some way to discern what is best.

Jeremiah was the Old Testament prophet with the calling we all admire but few of us would want. God gave him the difficult task of calling the nation of Israel to repentance and of demonstrating to the nation the hardships they would face under God's judgment. It was a strenuous calling that required unique training. As Jeremiah was trying to come to grips with God's plan for his life, God told him,

> "If you extract the precious from the worthless,
>   You will be my spokesman."
>   (Jeremiah 15:19 NASB)

It is strategic advice for all of us who want to be busy doing the best in our lives. To help you "extract the precious" that uncovers the unique purpose of your life, you'll want to ask questions that help you discover your passion, your uniqueness, your priority people, and your mission.

Discover Your Passion

What do you think about just before you go to bed and when you first wake up in the morning?

What issue recently made you righteously angry or brought you to tears?

Who or what are you willing to die for?

Who or what would you be willing to go to jail for, if the need arose?

What do you talk about the most?

Who or what are you willing to be inconvenienced for?

If you were guaranteed success and had unlimited funds, what would you want to do for God?[1]

Discover Your Uniqueness

What are three things you do well and enjoy doing?

What are three things you do not do well and do not enjoy doing?

What is unique about you? What do you do better than others? What do you do that is different from the activities of most of the people you know?

What are the repeating patterns in your experience? Write out five to seven short paragraphs of times you genuinely enjoyed or felt successful as you served others. After writing this down, highlight any repeating words, people groups, and circumstances.

What areas of your life are described by the statement, "Do first what only you can do?"

John Maxwell advises, "If someone can do what you do 80 percent as well as you, delegate it." Are there tasks or responsibilities you should or can delegate?

Discover Your Priority People

Who are the most important people in your life? Are they getting the time they need with you?

Fern Nichols notes, "Sometimes it is the right thing but the wrong time." Are there goals you need to put on hold to meet the current needs of the high-priority people in your life?

Patrick Morley caught our attention when he wrote, "Give your time away first to those who will cry at your funeral." Who are those people in your life? What can you do to spend appropriate time with them?

Discover Your Mission

What would you like said about you at your funeral? What legacy do you want to leave?

Have you selected a life verse? If so, write it in the space below. If not, begin looking for a verse that sums up what you hope God will do in your life.

Now use the answers to these questions to create a personal mission statement that can help focus your influence. Here are a few examples of other people's mission statements:

Bill is committed to help as many people as possible grow in their most important relationships, which include a relationship with God, family relationships, friendships, and people in their circle of influence.

Josh is committed to use his artistic gifts to help others get their message out.

Debe helps people grow closer to God through music, drama, poetry, crafts, and other worship experiences.

Charlie helps people understand themselves better. Through teaching, coaching, and personal discipleship, he helps others gain insight into their lives and how to live out their God-given purpose.

Give it a try. Use one of the following statements to help you get started with your mission statement:

I, _____ , commit to…

I, _____ , make it my mission to…

Create a Motto

By motto we mean a brief statement that summarizes your mission in a single sentence. Here are a few samples:

"Those who honor God, God honors" (1 Samuel 2:30).

"Do the right things for right reasons, and trust God for right results in the right time."

"Life is right when you worship."

"Helping you be you."

"Getting your message out to the world."

Give it a try. Write down the single sentence that comes to mind when you think about your mission:

Create an Emblem

Just as the Armed Forces or corporations have emblems or logos, see if you can create a piece of art that symbolizes those things you hold dearest. You might want to design it like a shield, a necklace, a framed art piece, a photo, or a screensaver. The goal is to create a daily reminder of what you want your life to stand for. Here is a picture of our family crest or emblem:

The three Ls down the center stand for our three main goals. We want to be Learners and Leaders who Love God. The cross with the star rising from it represents our conviction that everyone has a God-given dream, and when you find that dream, you will have plenty of motivation and energy. The two interlocking hearts represent our conviction to keep our promises. With integrity and commitment, we want to be known as people who do what they say they will do.

Give it a try. In the space below, draw a sketch of what you want your crest to look like. Remember, this is a brainstorming exercise, not an art assignment:

Now, pull together the pieces of this chapter and you have the makings of a great story. It's a story of God's faithfulness to you, and all He asks is that you are faithful to share and live out your story as a light to others. Tell your story for an audience of one or one million, wherever God calls. Just open your mouth and speak your story.

Just for Fun

Being faithful in life and faithful to tell your story involves yielding to Christ. Yielding is hard work. You have to stop, look, and listen before proceeding.

At a recent conference a couple was at our book table with their very hyper elementary-aged son. He was moving books and CDs and basically reshuffling the table.

Having raised sons myself, I (Pam) looked at the mom and simply said, "It's okay. They're just books. Don't worry."

Mom smiled gratefully, then turned to her husband and said, "I guess he has yielded long enough."

I loved how she phrased that and complimented her.

She replied in her sweet southern accent, "Oh dearie, that comes with a story. See my mima [grandma] was waiting at a yield sign, then she decided to go on through and was hit, plumb sideswiped hard by an oncoming car.

"When the officer asked her, 'Ma'am, why did you proceed through that yield sign?' she said, 'Well, I had just yielded long enough!'"

Keep yielding! Faithfulness comes with its perks.

CHAPTER 9

Decide to Be a Communicator

"The fruit of the Spirit is...gentleness."

Galatians 5:23

We're sure you've heard it before, "You need to learn to communicate." This is usually said in the midst of a tense conversation with one of your parents or a romantic interest. Talking about communication, therefore, is often not a happy experience since it is usually dressed in criticism and decorated with expectations. Communication, even with the best intentions can be a challenge, as some of these signs indicate:

> Spotted above a toilet in an office building: TOILET OUT OF ORDER. PLEASE USE FLOOR BELOW.

> In an office: AFTER TEA BREAK STAFF SHOULD EMPTY THE TEAPOT AND STAND UPSIDE DOWN ON THE DRAINING BOARD.

> Seen on a notice board: FOR ANYONE WHO HAS CHILDREN AND DOESN'T KNOW IT, THERE IS A DAY CARE CENTER ON THE FIRST FLOOR.

> On a repair shop door: WE CAN REPAIR ANYTHING. (PLEASE KNOCK HARD ON THE DOOR—THE BELL DOESN'T WORK.)

> On the counter at Pam's nail shop: NO CHICKS PLEASE.

Communication is one of the most powerful gifts we have been given. It is the door that opens up all the best possibilities of life or it is the spoiled ingredient that foments misunderstanding as it ruins relationships. As with most relationship skills, many people think communication is a talent you were either born with or not. But communication, like decision-making, is a skill that can be acquired and developed.

To illustrate the power of communication for both good and bad, consider the following stories from the Book of Acts. These stories take place in an intense time in the history of the church. The church had just been born in the midst of heavy opposition, with Saul (who would later become known as Paul) a lead antagonist. He was the most feared enemy of the church having devoted himself to arresting as many believers as possible and sentencing them to death. He was religiously motivated and totally committed. Then, Saul meets the risen Jesus, and his life is dramatically transformed (Acts 9:1-19).

But given Saul's reputation, we are not surprised to read a few verses later that, "When he came to Jerusalem, he tried to join the disciples, but they were all afraid of him, not believing that he really was a disciple" (9:26). Can you imagine Saul and the church resolving this without the ability to communicate? Only skilled sincere conversation could bridge the gap to welcome Saul into the fellowship of believers. This is where Barnabas comes in. Barnabas "took [Saul] and brought him to the apostles. He told them how Saul on his journey had seen the Lord and that the Lord had spoken to him, and how in Damascus he had preached fearlessly in the name of Jesus" (v. 27). Barnabas's skill introduced the greatest church planter in history to the infant church. Without mature, persuasive interaction, the church would most likely have continued to be afraid of one its greatest leaders.

This is a great reminder for all of us. Poor communication could have excluded one of the vital leaders in church history. People today are often excluded from our churches and circle of friends because of a lack of communication. We are all uncomfortable around people who are different from us because we fear what we don't understand. The only way to bridge these misunderstandings is through patient, persistent communication. Most of the people we find awkward are simply immature in their people skills and can be trained and encouraged to have quality relationships.

Paul is a great reminder that you can't tell a person's potential simply by what you see today.

The challenges continue in Acts 11. Peter has just returned from his encounter with Cornelius, the first Gentile convert to Christianity. The idea of non-Jewish people being part of the church was shocking to the other church leaders. They felt Peter had compromised his convictions and watered down the Word of God. Again, imagine that the people involved could not communicate. They were sincere. They were concerned. They were looking for answers, but it was all useless intention without the ability to communicate back and forth.

The interaction that occurred between them demonstrates three elements necessary for successful interpersonal communication.

Key Elements of Successful Communication

Open

The first element of any successful communication is the opening statement. Someone has to begin the conversation, but the opening statement is seldom based on full knowledge of a situation. Communication is necessary because no single person has the complete story. Peter's concerned friends began the conversation by confronting him: "You went into the house of uncircumcised men and ate with them" (Acts 11:3). None of those who now question Peter's actions were with him when Cornelius and his family were filled with the Holy Spirit. They are responding based on the knowledge they have. If they sit on the information, it will fester and turn into resentment, resistance, or further conflict. To get the conversation started, they share what they know.

Opening statements are usually based on limited insight. We know something is up, but we know only part of the story. This is where humility helps. If you are the one opening the discussion and you have the attitude, *I know something is up, but I am open to the possibility that I don't have it figured out,* that will go a long way toward fostering better understanding. Investigation is necessary before you reach a conclusion.

Options

The second element is the response. We have options for the ways we will respond. "Peter began and explained everything to them precisely as it had happened" (Acts 11:4). He could have been defensive and blurted out, "Hey, you weren't there and you didn't see what happened. You guys are out of control. I am out of here!" and then stormed out of the room. Instead, he patiently and enthusiastically reported with strategic details what happened. He shared the order of events, his own astonishment at what he saw, and the most important moment of his experience. Peter cannot control the reaction he will get from his friends, but he can make sure they base their feedback on full information.

Optimize

The third element is change. Successful communication always produces some change in us. It will optimize our future. We are limited and always learning. Part of our growth process comes from interacting with others. So every conversation moves us forward in some direction. Our hearts may soften or they may harden. We may grow in wisdom or reject the information. We may adjust our perspective with the new information or stubbornly refuse to bend our previous conclusions. In some way, however, we will be different after the conversation. Healthy interaction takes place when everyone involved receives the information with a soft and willing heart.

When Peter's friends heard this, "they had no further objections and praised God" (Acts 11:18). They started out concerned and ended up changed men. They shared Peter's astonishment and opened their minds to accept that Gentiles were as much the objects of God's grace as were Jewish believers. Prior to this conversation, they could not even imagine the possibility. After the conversation, they enthusiastically accepted what they previously believed was impossible. It's a good reminder to all of us that any conversation might be an interaction that changes our lives as effective interaction solves problems, opens our hearts, helps us grow, and exposes our weaknesses. The better your skills, the more likely communication will work for you in a positive way.

What You Say by What You Do

Much of communication is nonverbal. Your body language often says more to others than the words you say. If others are paying attention to your body language, they can tell a lot about you:

- They can tell if you are angry.
- They can sense your emotions.
- They can tell if you are trying to intimidate them.
- They can discern your attitude.
- They can tell when your attitude has improved.
- They can tell when you have had a significant spiritual experience.
- They can tell when you are sincere.
- They can tell if you respect them.
- They can tell when your heart is filled with joy.
- They can tell if there is romantic attraction.

Let Your Body Talk

Most of us are accidental in our body language. We simply do what we do without thinking about the message we're conveying. When you consider that much of the message you communicate is based on your body language, it makes sense to think through what your body is saying. Here are a few simple truths about body language to keep in mind.

The smaller your audience, the smaller your motions should be. If you are speaking to a large group, you'll want to stand up, use large hand motions, and cover enough space on the stage to engage the crowd. If you are engaged in a private conversation, you'll want to keep your hands closer to your body and use smaller motions as you communicate.

Large motions in close proximity give one of two messages. You are either insecure and trying to make sure the other person doesn't get too close or you are trying to intimidate the other person to gain an advantage. Smaller body motions, however, give the message that you are sincerely interested in the other person and you are comfortable in the current setting. You may actually feel uncomfortable, but if you choose your hand motions and body posture, you can give the impression to others that you are secure, which will draw healthier people to you.

You project interest when you lean toward another person. If you want others to know you are interested in what they are saying, gently lean forward. The same is true if you turn toward the other person so the communication is more eye to eye. Turning your back, walking away, or looking elsewhere when communicating sends the clear signal, "I am busy with things more important than you right now."

However, when you put down what is in your hands, look away from other distractions, and turn your chair toward the person, this says, "I am listening. I want to hear what you have to say, and it is safe to share. I will gently accept what you say and guard your heart in the process."

You want to be careful that you gently lean rather than lean in like an interrogator. If you lean too far, others will feel as if you are probing for information rather than sharing a conversation. As you talk with others, look for the angle that makes people comfortable around you.

You give a message of safety when you open up your posture. If you are sitting with your arms and your legs crossed, you make it clear that you are not really open to a conversation. Others will sense that you would rather be doing something else. If your hands are resting on your legs and both your legs are parallel to the floor, others will sense that you are interested in the conversation at hand. If your hands are in front of your mouth, you give the message that you are uncomfortable and are holding back. If your hands are resting comfortably on an armrest or on the back of a couch, you appear relaxed and calm.

This applies to meetings at work as well. If you meet with someone while you are behind your desk, you are creating distance, which may be strategic to getting an authoritative point across or it may express insecurity if the conversation is more casual. If you are meeting around a table, you will set people at ease if your hands are on the table rather than crossed in front of your chest.

These are simple things, but everything you do sends a message. The more aware you are of the message, the more strategic you can be in communicating with others.

Physical contact is a powerful force, so use it wisely. You can encourage others with a gentle touch or hug, but you can also create misunderstandings and awkwardness. People who are in affectionate physical contact with people they trust have lower heart rates, lower blood pressure, more relaxed muscles, and a general sense of well-being. It has such a powerful impact on us that we guard who we allow to touch us, and we often recoil from others when we are not ready to be touched.

The key is to internally define your relationships (as described in chapter 6) and monitor physical contact according to each relationship's definition. For instance, you might give a hug to a trusted friend but probably not to an acquaintance. You might high-five casual friends, but you probably wouldn't put your arm around their shoulder while giving advice.

As long as the physical contact is appropriate to the relationship, things are fine. If it doesn't match, things get weird.

Eye contact makes all the difference. You look at people you are interested in. Your eyes, more than any other part of your body, express what is going on in your heart. When you are ashamed, you avoid eye contact. When you are embarrassed, you avoid eye contact. When you are upset, you avoid eye contact. On the other hand, you will make eye contact when there is trust, appreciation, or fascination.

You need to be careful here because if you stare at another person, you will make him uncomfortable. You stare at people if you are interrogating them, and you stare at people if you lack social skills. The key is to make consistent eye contact. You'll want to look away often and then reengage eye contact. We have found that two seconds is about right. You can hold eye contact for about two seconds, look away, and then begin again. This way others will sense you are interested, but they won't feel probed.

You also want to concentrate on relaxing the muscles around your eyes. If you tense your eye muscles, your forehead will wrinkle, and you will give the impression that you disagree with what's being said.

Those of you who were raised in a healthy, safe home will instinctively know these things. If you were not raised in that kind of environment, it will take conscious effort to improve your body language. Even those who were raised in an emotionally healthy environment can get self-absorbed, stressed, or lazy and slack off using the body language that says, "You are valuable. You are worth my time and energy." Body language can say all that before a word is ever spoken.

Set Your Tone

The second most powerful component of communication is your tone of voice. Guess what kind of tone this exchange was given with?

> How many women with PMS does it take to screw in a light bulb? One. ONE! And do you know WHY it takes only ONE? Because no one else in this house knows HOW to change a light bulb. They don't even know the bulb is BURNED OUT. They would sit in this house in the dark for THREE DAYS before they figured it OUT. And once they figured it out, they wouldn't be able to find the light bulbs despite the fact that they've been in the SAME CUPBOARD for the past 17 YEARS. But if they did, by some miracle, find the light bulbs, TWO DAYS LATER the chair that they dragged from two rooms over to stand on to change the STUPID light bulb would STILL BE IN THE SAME SPOT! AND UNDERNEATH IT WOULD BE THE CRUMPLED WRAPPER THE STUPID LIGHT BULBS CAME IN. WHY? BECAUSE NO ONE IN THIS HOUSE EVER CARRIES OUT THE GARBAGE! IT'S A WONDER WE HAVEN'T ALL SUFFOCATED FROM THE PILES OF GARBAGE THAT ARE 12 FEET DEEP THROUGHOUT THE ENTIRE HOUSE. THE HOUSE! THE HOUSE! IT WOULD TAKE AN ARMY TO CLEAN THIS.[1]

Many homes today have an alarm system to protect them from intrusion and to alert the residents of the presence of smoke and carbon monoxide. When everything is okay, the system emits a variety of beeps and signals. These are the sounds that say, "Everything is okay. It's all right to roam freely around the house." When something is wrong in the house, the system lets out a shrill sound that disturbs everyone in the house.

Your interaction with others likewise has an alarm system that either announces that all is okay or disturbs everyone in the discussion. While body language may be the most important ingredient in your communication, the tone of your voice is not far behind in the influence it has on the climate of your relationships.[2] A gentle tone of voice will help people relax around you and engage in meaningful conversation. A harsh tone will create distance that leads to misunderstandings and conflict.

A gentle answer turns away wrath,
>   but a harsh word stirs up anger.
>   (Proverbs 15:1)

People do not think much about their tone of voice as they are growing up. From your earliest days, you reacted to the people you grew up around. They made you happy and you responded. They seemed unreasonable and you resisted. They were irritating and you reacted. These people had a profound impact on who you are today. It's possible that your skill in choosing your tone of voice from conversation to conversation developed well, but it is more likely that you simply reacted to what happened around you.

The tone in your voice will give people one of two impressions about you. Some tones will cause people to believe that you are gentle toward them. Your voice will reassure them that you care about them and that you are safe to talk with. Other tones give people the impression you are trying to gain control over them. Your voice will challenge them and persuade them that you are trying to get the upper hand in the conversation. Your agenda may not be clear to them, but they get the distinct impression that you do have an agenda that does not have their best interests in mind.

A tone of voice that tells people you are gentle will be characterized by:

- *Softness.* A soft voice calms everyone down.

- *Drop in inflection.* The inflection in your voice will go down a little at the end of your sentences. The trailing off of your voice expresses sincerity, making you more believable.

- *Appropriateness.* Interactions work best when the tone in your voice is appropriate for the conversation. Life is lived out in a variety of situations and surprises we must all react to. If your friend just received a promotion at work and you react with an affirming tone of voice, he will be encouraged. If there is a kitchen fire and you scream at your roommates to help, they will respond by jumping in.

A tone of voice that discourages healthy interaction is characterized by:

- *Loudness.* A loud voice will put people on the alert and cause them to take a defensive posture with you—unless you are carrying a message of thrill, excitement, or good news. People can handle a little more volume when the messenger is carrying positive news.

- *Harshness*. When there is a bite in your voice, the person you are talking with will become defensive. The introverts will shut down while the extroverts will argue with you.

- *Rise in inflection*. The inflection of your voice will rise at the end of a sentence. Other people will think you are selling something or trying to convince them of something.

- *Inappropriateness*. If you react to your friend's promotion with sadness, he will be confused. If you respond to the kitchen fire with a calm, soft voice, they will wonder what is wrong with you.

- *Other negative actions*. A negative tone is sometimes carried by short, choppy sentences or accompanied with sighs of exasperation or rolling of the eyes. Sometimes it is easier to catch yourself doing these actions even if you can't hear when your tone of voice changes from positive to negative. If you can't hear the difference, you can decide to quit flailing your arms, stomping your feet, rolling your eyes, or huffing in exasperation. If you curb those, chances are you will also curb your tone of voice. (Clue: If you were to write what you are saying and you used all CAPS, the tone would probably be negative if you said it aloud.)

You are generally the last one to be aware of your tone of voice. You are so attached to your life and your reactions to it that your senses grow dull when it comes to recognizing the influence of your voice. You can sharpen your senses by deliberately listening to yourself and asking, "How would I respond if my good friend used the tone of voice I just used?"

You can also ask someone you trust to evaluate your tone of voice for you. This could be your small group leader, a friend, or a trusted colleague at work. This works only if you give this person explicit permission to evaluate you. You can say something like, "For the next week, will you point out to me when I do well with my tone of voice and when I push people away with my tone?" Give a time limit so this doesn't become the definition of your relationship, and decide ahead of time that you will take what they say seriously. If not, you will become defensive rather than grow through their insight.

Emotions are primarily communicated through body language and tone of voice, so the actual words can be overrun by the nonverbals. Don't let that fool you, though. Your words may be small, but they are very important to the quality of your communication.

Conversations Based on Type of Relationship

All healthy relationships are defined. When you take the time to define the relationships in your life, it becomes much simpler to figure out the types of conversations that are appropriate. In other words, you want to choose your words based on the type of relationship you are dealing with.

Consider the following relationship hierarchy:

Relationship Hierarchy			
Level of Involvement	Type of Relationship		
	Friendships	*Work Relationships*	*Romantic Interests*
Cautious	Acquaintances	Acquaintances	Acquaintances
Curious	Casual Friends	Colleagues	Casual Dating
Confident	Trusted Friends	Trainees	Exclusive Dating
Connected	Mentors	Mentors	Fiancée
Committed			Husband/Wife

Cautious Conversations

When you are dealing with relationships that fall in the cautious category, you want to use guarded speech. You will want to intentionally keep conversations simple, shallow, and safe. With acquaintances you do not want to share your dreams, your fears, or your disappointments. It is fine to talk about vacations, hobbies, tasks at work, and anything about yourself that you would be willing to announce on a cable news program. If you share vulnerable truths about yourself with acquaintances, you will attract unhealthy people to yourself and be consistently disappointed by the friends you keep.

All relationships start at this level. When you meet someone new, you may be meeting a great friend, a mentor, or someone who should never be more than just an acquaintance. You can't tell at first if this person is weird or wonderful. It is helpful, therefore, to develop a routine for talking with people who are new in your life.

The best way to get a good impression of others is to ask simple questions about them. You don't have to be spontaneous with the questions you come up with. You can actually ask the same questions of everyone you meet. As they talk about themselves, you will form an initial impression of how healthy this person is. If you determine this individual would be a distraction in your life, you can keep the conversation very simple and severely limit future contact. If, however, your first impression is positive, you can continue the conversation and look for other opportunities to interact. As you think about meeting new people, decide ahead of time that you will ask these questions:

Five Questions to Ask in the
First Five Minutes of Meeting Someone New

1. What is your name?
2. How long have you been a part of this organization? church? group? (Never ask, "Are you new here?" If they are new, they are already feeling awkward about it. If they aren't, you will look stupid.)
3. Where do you work or go to school?
4. Who are the members of your family?
5. Where did you grow up?

Curious Conversations

Some of your acquaintances will progress to become friends, colleagues, and casual dating relationships. These are still very casual relationships, but you have determined that you have enough in common with these people that the relationship is worth investigating. You still don't know how much you can trust them with, but you like spending time with them and find value in your interactions.

With these friends, you'll want to progress to asking casual questions and sharing your preferences with one another. This is where you begin to talk about music and other entertainment options you prefer. You'll want to discuss free-time preferences, personal growth preferences, and simple problem-solving situations.

You still want to be cautious at this point because not all casual friends prove to be faithful and trustworthy. Therefore, you still do not want to open up about your hurts and fears or your most important dreams. Most of your casual friends will remain casual and cannot handle intimate knowledge about your past or your dreams. Be content to keep it casual and have fun with these people.

Confident Communication

The next level of relationships comes with the confidence to open up. You will meet people who become trusted friends, exclusive dating interests, and people who want you to mentor them in the workplace. These people rise to this level because they have proved themselves to be emotionally safe and socially enjoyable. They probably share your convictions and respect your privacy.

You can, therefore, explore more sensitive information. You can tell them about your dreams and the obstacles you have overcome. You can discuss the most significant steps of growth you have taken and the plans you intend to pursue next. You can also share from your areas of expertise with freedom and enthusiasm since these people respect you and want to learn from you.

You just want to be careful about being too needy with these people. You will have good give-and-take with them, but they are not in a position to instruct you, lead you, or compassionately accept you in spite of your weaknesses. Just enjoy these relationships, laugh with them often, and ask them for advice in all but the most sensitive areas of your life.

Connected Communication

Along your journey, you may meet a few people who qualify to be truly connected with you. The most common are mentors. These people have developed proficiencies that you desire and the character to be trusted with anything you need to share to move forward in life. They have proven themselves to you and can be trusted at the deepest levels. As a result, they are very influential and help you become a better person. They may be mentors who help you get better in a specific area or they may be general mentors you want to learn from in multiple areas.

Some of you may also discover someone you will consider spending the rest of your life with. As you date seriously and move toward engagement, you will want to explore the possibilities of the relationship by sharing the deep things of your life to ensure you can trust this person with the stuff that most people don't know. The agonizingly slow areas of growth, the hurts from your past, and the disappointments that have left you scarred need to be shared to give you the confidence that you can live with each other for the rest of your lives. You can hide these things from those who don't live in your home, but they will be exposed when you share the same address.

Committed Communication

There is one relationship that stands apart from all the others, and we call it marriage. We know marriage is beyond the scope of this book, but it must be mentioned to maintain perspective.

When you get married, you share everything in life with one person. You share your schedules, your money, your decisions, your children, your bodies, your fears, and your victories. This relationship is supported best when there is courageous, committed conversation. Any subject can come up at any time. You will surprise each other with secrets you have kept from everyone else, and you will disappoint each other with your imperfections.

Without unconditional commitment, this can be frightening. With lifelong, encouraging commitment, this can be one of the greatest experiences in life. If this kind of relationship comes your way, make the most of it. If not, don't force it. Just enjoy the freedom of having lots of good friends.

RAISE the Bar

It's easy to break down the different types of relationships and talk about what kind of words are appropriate, but we all know that relationships don't follow scripts and they don't stay in neat categories. Sometimes, you just have to respond to the situation at hand. You will navigate these situations better if you have chosen guidelines ahead of time to guide your words in any situation.

You will find appropriate words in any situation if you decide to RAISE the bar as you communicate with others. These words will create a safety net that will make you approachable while at the same time making unhealthy people uncomfortable around you. Words that RAISE a verbal safety net on your relationships include:

Respect. Everyone you meet has been made in the image of God and is, therefore, deserving of respect. Because all people are at different levels of maturity, some people are easier to respect than others. Giving respect, however, is more about who you are than who they are. If you believe everyone has value, you will find a way to respect them. If you believe everyone has a unique contribution to make, you will find a way to respect them. If you believe everyone is in the process of growth and has potential to be more than they are today, you will find a way to give respect.

Healthy people respond positively to statements of respect that include sincere compliments, requests for advice, appreciation for their input, and friendly challenges to put their talents into action. Unhealthy people find these statements to be intimidating because they are given with the expectation of increased responsibility and maturity. It isn't that unhealthy people run away the first time you talk with them, but over time they will discover that you run at a faster pace and pursue bigger goals than they are willing to consider.

Affirmation. Everyone is good at something. Many people have been wounded and hurt, so they hold back or have grown overly cautious, but they still have talent. Pointing out this talent gives people an opportunity to get on or stay on the path of growth. We live in a tough world, so everyone faces obstacles in their pursuits. Sometimes an honest affirmation from you helps others refocus.

"I" statements. Most conversations go better when you speak about

your conclusions and the way life is affecting you. The tendency is to point out what you believe the other person is thinking or the behavior you don't like in the other person. Both of these tendencies breed defensiveness.

"I really enjoyed the concert at church last weekend," is better than, "Didn't you enjoy the concert at church?" The first statement gives others a clear path to engage you in conversation. They can either agree with you or have a different opinion. The second statement makes them feel as though you are thinking for them rather than starting a conversation.

"For some reason, it is very upsetting to me when we arrive late," is much different than, "You make me so mad because you are always late." Both statements make it clear that you would like to see something change. The first statement allows the other person to safely enter the conversation. The second encourages that person to put up defenses.

Sincerity. We are told in the Bible to "speak the truth in love" (Ephesians 4:15). Whatever you say to other people, you want it to be the truth. You don't want to make up statements just to be nice. You also are not responsible for any changes that ought to happen in others, so you don't have to point out everything that is true. The key is to sincerely share words that help this relationship be what it is. If it is casual, be casual. If it is connected relationship, share deeper. You want to be sincere so you don't ever have to explain later why you said what you didn't mean.

Encouragement. Give sincere compliments; look for ways to build up others. "Encourage one another and build each other up" is a choice God challenges us to make daily (1 Thessalonians 5:11; Hebrews 3:13). It is a picture of building a solid home and sheltering it with a reliable roof. As you get comfortable with encouraging others, you become a safe person who helps others be their best. Friendship circles made up of people who are functioning well are fun to be a part of, and you can help create this type of circle with sincere, consistent compliments.

Awkward, Weird, and Strange

Conversations can be like a dropped cell call. You're not sure if you should call back or just walk away. Some conversations can just go haywire on you.

Jeff was visiting his girlfriend's home when he realized the battery in his beat-up VW Beetle had died because he left the lights on. Jeff explains his interaction with his girlfriend:

> I was in a hurry to get to work on time, so I ran into the house to get my girlfriend to give me a hand starting the car.
>
> I told her to get into her car—a huge, oversized gas guzzling pickup truck—and use it to push my car fast enough to start it. I pointed out to her that because the VW had an automatic transmission, it needed to be pushed at least 30 mph for it to start.
>
> She said fine, hopped into her truck, and drove off.
>
> I sat there fuming, wondering what she could be doing and where she was going. A minute passed, and when I saw her in the rearview mirror coming at me at about 40 mph, I realized I should have been a bit clearer with my directions!

Regrouping for Reconnection

We all bring our hopes, dreams, desires, and emotions to relationships. As a result, it is common to periodically feel awkward around other people. Sometimes this weirdness is positive because the relationship is so valuable to you. You may be spending time with a mentor, a personal hero, or a romantic interest. These people mean so much to you that you become self-conscious and overly concerned about your actions and words. Other times, the awkward feeling is negative because you just don't want to be around a person who may be overbearing, demanding, or just plain creepy. Being in this person's presence feels weird.

Part of growing as a communicator is to learn what to say when the weirdness sets in. To help you focus at these times, review the following:

10 Things to Say When You Don't Know What to Say

1. "Excuse me. I will be back in a few minutes." This is useful when you need to take a break. "A few minutes" is better than "I will be right back" because it sets different expectations.

2. "I need to go but it was good spending time with you."

3. "I need some time to think about that. If you need an answer right now, I'm afraid the answer will be no. If you want to give me time to think about it, I'll give you a more measured response. Let me pray about that."

4. "I am sorry for doing…" Be specific if you use this one. Vague apologies are obnoxious and ruin friendships. For example, "If I have done anything to hurt your feelings, I am sorry," is an accusation about the other person being thin-skinned or dimwitted. It is not an apology.

5. Ask questions. People love to talk about themselves, so questions tend to open up conversation. Your questions might include, "What is your favorite hobby?" "When was your last vacation?" "Have you learned anything recently that fascinated you?" "Have you read any books lately you would recommend to me?" As the other person answers, more questions will probably rise to the surface.

6. "Can you help me with…" or "I'd love to hear what you think about…" This is effective if you enjoy the other person's company. People love to be needed, so asking for their help makes them feel important and tends to open up new conversation. If you are uncomfortable around this person, you do not want to employ this one!

7. "I would love to do that." When someone suggests something that you would get enthusiastic about, let them know.

8. "Wow, that is an interesting thought. I can't picture this for myself, but thanks for sharing it." If you don't agree or you cannot picture what they are talking about as at all healthy for you, share your feelings and try not to judge theirs. We all tend to be judgmental about activities others engage in that would not be good for us. When you make a value judgment, you often become the issue rather than the unhealthy decisions of others. When you keep the focus on your

decision rather than theirs, you maintain healthy boundaries and protect your self-respect. You should feel free to voice your opinion and share your choices, just make them from your point of view: "I feel…" "I have found…" I prefer…"

9. "I really appreciate…" Follow this statement with a sincere compliment. Too often we withhold encouragement when it is exactly what the conversation needs. When you appreciate something about another individual, you give off nonverbal clues. The other person doesn't know what those clues mean, so they start to guess. When you speak the compliment, it takes the mystery out and allows an honest and sincere response.

10. "I need to share something important with you." You might need to set some boundaries or distance, which is extremely difficult. Word the conversation something like this: "This is hard for me to tell you, and I am sure harder for you to hear, but until this changes (describe the specific unhealthy behavior), I cannot spend time with you." This is reserved for truly unhealthy people who are trying to befriend you. You want to make it clear that their behavior is unacceptable to you without taking any responsibility for the change that would benefit them.

Really good communication is like mocha—rich like chocolate and addictive like caffeine. Once you have tasted great conversation, terrific storytelling, and authentic sharing, it's hard to settle for anything less. Be the leader in your circle of influence who sets the bar on great communication. Model for others how you like to be related to, and soon others will mirror your wise choices.

Just for fun

A couple came into the pastor's office for some premarital counseling. They had been arguing and needed to resolve their communication problems. The fighting and bickering during the session was so bad, the pastor called for a timeout and told them he was ending the session early but had an assignment for the boyfriend.

"John," the pastor said, "you're an athletic guy. Here's what I want you to do. I want you to jog 10 miles every day for the next 30 days. At the end of the 30 days, call me and let me know how things are going."

John agreed.

At the end of the 30 days, John called the pastor very excited. "I did just as you said, and I have never felt better in my life!"

"Great!" the pastor said. "And how are things going with your girl-friend?"

John paused and then replied with agitated dismay, "How should I know? I'm 300 miles from home!"

CHAPTER 10

Decide to Be a Competitor

"The fruit of the Spirit is...self-control."

GALATIANS 5:23

Before you react to the title of this chapter, this is not just for athletes. It is based on the fact that life is competitive and can be mastered only by those willing to compete. We compete spiritually against the forces of darkness. We compete against the elements to maintain our homes and our health. We compete against others to develop our careers. And we compete against our own desires in order to live strong, satisfying lives.

The Bible gives a number of analogies to help us gain perspective on what life is really like. These word pictures are designed to prepare us for the rigors of accomplishing the purpose God has designed us for.

Fight the Good Fight

The most common picture in the New Testament for a follower of Christ is that of a soldier. In 2 Corinthians 10:3, Paul boldly says, "For though we live in the world, we do not wage war as the world does." Notice that being in the skirmish is not an option, but how we engage in battle is one of the key choices of life. A number of characteristics of soldiers are instructive in helping us figure out how to live strategically in a world that is trying to keep us down.

Soldiers of Christ get dressed for battle. Ephesians 6 describes our preparation for life in the same way soldiers prepare for the battlefield.

The goal of putting on battledress is to maintain strength. We don't prepare ourselves just to be busy. The goal is to "be strong in the Lord and in his mighty power" (v. 10). When we talk about getting dressed for battle, we aren't referring to a uniform; this is a different kind of battle. "Our struggle is not against flesh and blood, but against the rulers, against the authorities, against the powers of this dark world and against the spiritual forces of evil in the heavenly realms" (v. 12). In other words, our struggle is primarily a spiritual one.

The world system we operate in is highly influenced by evil and ungodly priorities. The spiritual atmosphere of the world is polluted with the presence of evil spirits and false teaching. Finally, our own souls are plagued by our old natures, which are hostile to God's ways and selfishly focused. These are enemies that must be subdued if we are going to be free to live out our dream.

Armor for Stability

The first goal of the armor is to *create stability*: "with the belt of truth buckled around your waist" (v. 14). A Roman soldier's armor was attached to his belt to keep it in place during travel and battle. Likewise, your personal intake of the truth of Scripture is crucial for your spiritual stability. The truth you learn through your interaction with God's Word provides stable places in your life to keep the rest of your spiritual armor in place when it is needed the most.

You can infuse the truth of the Bible into your life in numerous ways, and it takes consistency in all of these to maintain the spiritual and intellectual resources you need to make great decisions. Romans 10:17 reveals that part of the process of buckling up is *hearing* the Bible: "Faith comes from hearing." You can accomplish this through listening to others teach God's Word, attending church regularly where God's Word is preached, or investing in an audio Bible.

The second notch on the belt is *reading* the Bible. In Deuteronomy 17:18-19 the king of Israel was commanded to keep a copy of God's Word with him, and he was to "read it all the days of his life." First Thessalonians 5:27 is a New Testament example of the priority of reading the Bible as part of our spiritual journey: "I charge you before the Lord to have this letter read to all the brothers." As you read the Bible regularly, you put together the pieces of the puzzle as you see how the Old and New Testaments are tied together and how the principles of God's Word are consistent from cover to cover.

Second Timothy 2:15 reminds us that *studying* is the third notch that helps us secure the belt of truth. When the Bible was written, the authors used the common language of the day so that it would be readily understandable to common men. It was, however, written in a different time and different culture than we live in. To harvest the principles taught so that we can integrate them into our lives, we need to diligently investigate the truth of God's Word and the cultural setting in which it was penned.

Psalm 119:11 reveals that *memorizing* is the fourth notch on the belt of truth. Righteous living develops when you hide God's Word in your heart through committing it to memory. This gets harder as we get older, but it never loses its importance.

To finish cinching the belt up, Psalm 1 challenges us to *meditate* on God's Word "day and night." Meditation is the process of thinking over and over about what we have learned. The more you focus on truth, the clearer it becomes. The more you wrestle with how to live it out in your life, the more skilled you get at living a biblical lifestyle.

So these five notches on the belt of truth keep it secure in your life: hearing, reading, studying, memorizing, and meditating.

It's not enough, however, to just take in truth. Hebrews 4:12 tells us that the Word of God is "living and active." Just as a soldier does not put on his uniform just to take pictures, we don't put on the belt of truth just to admire its beauty. The Word of God "judges the thoughts and attitudes of the heart" and calls us to action. As we infuse the Bible into our lives, a reaction begins within our souls that is designed to help us grow. We need to pay attention to God's Word as we immerse ourselves in it.

This interactive nature of the Bible causes it to affect us in two distinct ways.

Verses that encourage us. The first are verses that make us feel better about ourselves and about our lives. God uses these verses to keep us encouraged in the midst of the struggle. He knows that life is difficult and that we often get worn down and worn out, and He wants us to be reminded that He is always with us, always engaged in our journey, and always committed to "cause all things to work together for good to those who love God" (Romans 8:28). He, therefore, causes certain verses to jump off the pages of Scripture to encourage our hearts.

Verses that bother us. But certain verses we read can elicit some kind of disturbing reaction. We may be confused or irritated or agitated by what we read. The reason we have this reaction is that this passage is pointing to an area in our life that God wants to change. An attitude or an action or a habit may be next on God's agenda for change in our life. He knows the time is right, so He begins to stir up our soul in preparation for another transforming experience.

We often ignore these verses because they are uncomfortable. We assume we don't have the ability to understand or that Satan is trying to confuse us, when in reality God is trying to get our attention for the next step of maturity. The other reason we often ignore these verses is that they aren't clear to us. Even though the passage points to an area of growth, it may not point directly at the change. For instance, if God needs to toughen us up, stories of judgment and confrontation may bother us. Or if God wants to soften us up, we may find stories of compassion and intimacy unattractive and irritating.

The key is to pay attention to any verses you have a reaction to. When you commit to do this every time you are aware of it, Jesus becomes the instructor who helps you skillfully integrate truth into your life. He lets you know when change is necessary. He lets you know when you can relax and enjoy the progress you've already made. He lets you know when it's time to step up the intensity and focus on strenuous obedience. He points out when a bad habit is stifling your effectiveness and how to make the changes that remove the limits to your success.

Buckle Up

Make a note here of verses that you are reacting to.

Verses that have been encouraging to me:

Verses that have been bothering me:

Armor for Protection

The second step in preparing for battle is to *protect your heart*. The breastplate covered soldiers' chests so that weapons could not reach their hearts. They knew that once the heart stops, life stops, so they took great care to protect it.

Spiritually it is the same way. Proverbs 4:23 states, "Above all else, guard your heart, for it is the wellspring of life." In a spiritual sense, your heart gives you ability to love God, love others, and speak words of value. Your heart gives you energy for life and makes you more interesting than a robot.

Putting on the breastplate of righteousness is not a self-willed attempt to do what is right. It begins with trusting Jesus for your salvation. He paid the price for your mistakes and is willing to give His righteousness to you. He will represent you when you stand before God at judgment, and He will give you the Holy Spirit to give you the power you need to make righteous decisions. So the key to protecting your heart is to develop a vibrant, interactive relationship with Christ.

The next step is to *stand firm* "with your feet fitted with the readiness that comes from the gospel of peace." Roman soldiers wore footwear that had spikes or cleats on the bottom. The goal was to maintain firm footing in the midst of attacks. When they were fending off the blows of a sword, soldiers did not want to fall down. They were determined to stay on their feet to keep any advantage they could find.

Peace does this for us, and it comes in two forms. The first is *relational peace*, the realization that "there is now no condemnation for those who are in Christ Jesus" (Romans 8:1). God is not mad at you. God will not reject you. You will be accepted at judgment and live in the presence of God forever. In a word, you are okay. The second is *experiential peace*. This is a gift God gives as you interact with Him. Philippians 4:6-7 informs us that "the peace of God, which transcends all understanding, will guard your hearts and your minds in Christ Jesus." This is the calmness that God brings to help us maintain composure during the surprises and setbacks that interrupt our lives.

The shield of faith is the primary source of protection for a soldier in battle. Roman soldiers went on the battlefield with a shield large enough to crouch behind. When the enemy launched fire-tipped arrows, these soldiers would settle in behind their shield and let it absorb the shots. Once the enemy ran out of arrows, he would emerge from behind the shield and go into action.

In the same way, falsehoods and seductive temptations are launched at us daily. They are attractive and appear to be useful to reduce stress, give direction, or raise our confidence. In reality, they are fiery arrows that will pierce our hearts and render us useless in the most important pursuits of life.

The shield is made up of faith, which is a commitment in our hearts that God's Word is true. It is not just an intellectual conclusion. If we truly believe the truth of God's Word, we will live it out. If we have faith that God's will for us is to "give thanks in everything" (1 Thessalonians 5:18), then we will give thanks to God regardless of our circumstances. If we believe the path to greatness is humble servanthood (Matthew 23:11), we will serve others.

The final defensive piece of armor is the helmet of salvation. Roman soldiers commonly fought with heavy swords. One of the most effective moves was to raise the sword in the air and swing it down on the head of your enemy. To ward off this type of attack, soldiers wore a metal helmet that was slanted on both sides so the sword would glance off.

Spiritually, salvation protects our minds so we think straight and recognize truth: "The mind controlled by the Spirit is life and peace; the sinful mind is hostile to God" (Romans 8:6-7). In other words, salvation helps us think straight. People who have not met Jesus get caught up in ideas that sound good but don't work. They hear the truth but don't recognize it as true. When Jesus regenerates our souls, He also gives clarity to our minds so we don't fall prey to the deceptive ideas from the world around us.

This is the only way to explain what we see going on with our country's finances. The national debt is spiraling out of control, yet politicians continue to spend more money. Anyone who has lived on a budget knows you need to spend less money than you bring in. Common sense tells us that we can't live indefinitely on debt. People with power, however, are caught up in their self-perpetuating importance and can't find the will to do what is obvious to the rest of us. There is no other option than for this thinking to eventually lead to our self-destruction, but the people in charge don't seem to be able to see this simple truth.

Before we become too critical of our politicians, let's remember that we are all susceptible to thinking that doesn't fit reality. People regularly spend money they don't have, entertain themselves with ideas they don't believe, hang out with unhealthy people, and look for happiness in money, relationships, and hobbies. We honestly believe these things will work even though they have never worked before. When we walk with Jesus, however, we have the mind of Christ to work with so that we can be transformed by the renewing of our minds (1 Corinthians 2:16; Romans 12:2).

Our Only Weapon

Once we have our uniform on, we're ready to go into action. The one offensive part of our spiritual armor is "the sword of the Spirit, which is the word of God" (Ephesians 6:17).

The Bible is not just another book. It's a powerful weapon for breaking down deception, bringing wisdom to confusing situations, and driving away forces that seek to defeat you. As a result, you want to work it naturally into your life. Whenever you have a decision to make, create the habit of finding one or two verses that apply to that situation. Start with easy decisions, then grow into finding verses for more complicated ones.

Whenever you are afraid, read the Bible out loud. Sometimes fear exists because of the presence of evil spirits. When you announce the truth out loud, these enemies find somewhere else to go. At other times you sense fear because you're facing something big in life. God's Word will remind you that you are victorious in Christ and that you have a Savior who will never leave you nor forsake you.

Your Bible is one of your most valuable assets as you take your journey in life. You don't have to be weird about it and quote verses in every conversation, just as a soldier doesn't pull out his sword every time he says hello to someone. But you want to have the truth of Scripture ready to use when you need it.

A Soldier's Authority

Everyone who competes in life exercises authority and lives under authority. We unexpectedly encounter this in Matthew 8. Jesus has been traveling around Galilee doing ministry. As He returned to His hometown of Capernaum, He was approached by a centurion whose servant was "home paralyzed and in terrible suffering" (v. 6). Jesus' reputation for compassionate and miraculous healing was becoming well known, so this soldier approached the Master to see if He could find a solution for his servant. Jesus compassionately offered to go with the man to fulfill his request.

The centurion's response gives great insight into what it means to compete as a soldier. First, he recognized the superior authority of Jesus: "Lord, I do not deserve to have you come under my roof" (v. 8). He trusted Christ could do what he requested because he respected the power and authority Jesus had previously demonstrated. The centurion knew he was an influential, important man, but compared to Jesus, he was a simple servant.

This is one of the secrets to success in a competitive world. Each of us is talented and capable, but we all have people in authority over us.

First and foremost, Jesus has the authority to direct our lives in whatever way He pleases. He is kind and gentle in His leadership, but He is still the leader. He can call us into action, tell us to wait, direct us to train, or put us in charge. Saying yes to Jesus is, therefore, the key to competition.

In the commitments of our life, we find ourselves under other people's authority also. We submit to our governing officials, our bosses, and our church leaders. When we refuse to submit to the legitimate authority around us, we stifle our growth and limit opportunities.

The centurion continued, "But just say the word, and my servant will be healed. For I myself am a man under authority, with soldiers under me. I tell this one, 'Go,' and he goes; and that one, 'Come,' and he comes. I say to my servant, 'Do this,' and he does it" (vv. 8-9). This officer tells Jesus that he is able to direct the affairs of others because of the position he has attained. In the same way, he is convinced that all Jesus has to do is say the word and his servant will be healed. He understood that those who willingly live under authority get to exercise authority to influence those around them.

The goal of this process is to help build a network of success. The centurion served to help his commander succeed. He worked hard, set goals, and followed through with commitments to assist his leaders in the pursuit of their goals. Similarly, he directed those under his authority so they could succeed in their responsibilities. Without direction, they would have no idea what was expected of them or how they were supposed to carry out their duties. When the centurion gave clear directions, those under his charge could operate effectively.

You may not be in the military, but the principle is the same. God has given you opportunities to help those above and those below you to be more successful than they would be without your help.

Get It Done

Take a moment right now to answer the following questions:

> What can I do this week to help those who lead me to be more successful?

> What can I do this week to help those who are under my leadership to be more successful?

Train to Win

The next most prominent word picture in the Bible to describe followers of Jesus is that of athlete. All of our sons are athletes, and I married a woman who was a college athlete. I was an athlete, although sometimes I'm a legend in my own mind. I would have played in the NBA except I was too short, too slow, and my shot was too off. If not for that, I would have been awesome.

A few years ago, I watched the slam-dunk contest during the NBA All-Star weekend with two of my sons, ages 12 and 10 at the time. Afterward, we were driving around town running errands when my 10-year-old asked, "Dad, how tall is that guy who was slam dunking?"

"His name is Spud Webb, and he's 5 feet 7 inches tall."

"How tall are you, Dad?"

"I'm 5 feet 11 inches tall."

"Well, how come you can't slam dunk? Are you too fat?"

I was about to respond when my oldest son chimed in, "Zachery, Dad is not too fat. He weighs the same as Michael Jordan."

I thought I was raising a genius until he added, "Dad is not too fat. He's just too old."

Ouch! I'm glad God's version of an athlete is one we can all succeed at.

Paul uses the athlete analogy to raise the intensity level of his challenge to the believers in Corinth. In 1 Corinthians 9, he has been establishing the integrity of his calling. He has had to cover some tough subjects in previous chapters, such as fidelity in marriage, not being a stumbling block to others, lawsuits, and immoral behavior. You can imagine that some people were wondering, "Who is this guy that he can confront us on all of this?"

Well, Paul takes time to tell them, and then he shares the attitude behind his energy: "Do you not know that in a race all the runners run, but only one gets the prize? Run in such a way as to get the prize" (v. 24). He tells these beloved friends, "I intend to win in life. I am not just playing around. I'm seeking to be the best I can be at what I do best." The implication is that everyone ought to live this way. It's almost as if Paul is saying, "If you enter the race, of course you want to win it."

He then reminds us all of what it takes to get there.

Love the Game

First and foremost, you must love the privilege of being a part of God's plan. Paul says, "I do all this for the sake of the gospel, that I may share in its blessings" (1 Corinthians 9:23). Paul didn't struggle with motivation because he loved what he did. He considered the gospel the most valuable thing on earth, and being a part of God's plan was the greatest privilege he could imagine.

This is the way athletes feel. They compete because they love it. It gets in their blood and drives them. The possibility of being on the team and in the game makes their whole life more vibrant and energetic. It requires long hours and strenuous effort; they get sore, tired, and frustrated. Year after year, however, athletes compete because they love the game. They will pay whatever price is necessary, and they always keep their eye on the goal of winning the next contest.

I (Pam) love to kayak. Recently I was kayaking in Alaska where they have the "50/50 rule," which means that if you are 50 feet from shore and you capsize, you have a 50/50 chance of surviving. The wind came up on the lake and the waves were getting higher and higher, so we had to make it to shore and to safety as fast as we could. Our guide said to us, "Ladies, this is going to hurt, maybe hurt a lot. If you do not press in and press on, it will be dangerous. So if you want to make it home alive, dig in and push."

Well, we women dug in. We were all over 40; some were as old as 68. But we pushed, pressed, and persevered against the wind and rain and waves to make it to shore.

I have seen Bill, who loves to run, outrun a crocodile and outmaneuver an attacking long-beaked bird, pressing forward on his morning run despite the obstacles. We all push forward for the love of the game, the enjoyment of the activity, and the thrill of the finish.

Do you love life? Does the possibility of success thrill you? Do you still feel the sense of satisfaction when you finish a project, close a deal, overcome a problem, or create a breakthrough? Does the potential of earning more, having a bigger slice of influence, or helping others figure out who they are get to you?

We hope so because that is how God created you. God gave you a heart so that you could love Him, love life, and love the important people in your world. We are all born with a love for life. Just watch kids playing some time. They are determined to have fun, they are curious without hesitation, they laugh and cry without shame, and they run into the arms of people they recognize. They dream of greatness and worlds far, far away. In short, they love life.

We were like that once. Then we grow up, and if we are not careful, we lose our zest for life amidst the disappointments, defeats, and difficulties.

Focus on Victory

Athletes have the ability to maintain intense focus because they dream of winning. They picture their performances ahead of time and imagine a favorable outcome. They either see themselves winning the race, leading at the end of the game, setting a new record, or reaching a new level of accomplishment. Athletes in every sport compete because they want to win on game day.

Life is the same way. God has called us to live in victory, and it begins with our focus. Winners think like winners.

Hebrews 12:1-4 presents the journey of life as an athletic competition. There is a crowd in the stands (saints who have lived before us) cheering us on, and there is a focal point for the race. In this case it is a person: "Let us fix our eyes on Jesus, the author and perfecter of our faith, who for the joy set before him endured the cross, scorning its shame, and sat down at the right hand of the throne of God" (v. 2). First Corinthians 15:57 declares, "But thanks be to God! He gives us the victory through our Lord Jesus Christ." In Philippians 3:14, Paul reveals the secret that keeps him going: "I press on toward the goal to win the prize for which God has called me heavenward in Christ Jesus."

These verses all remind us that victory begins in the mind. If you can envision your dream, you can live it. If you can imagine a life worth living, you can pull the pieces together to make it happen. If you keep the goal in focus, you can figure out much easier the strategy that leads to victory.

Competitors lose their enthusiasm when they forget why they're in the game. When you have a clear goal, you gain the energy to pursue victory. This has proved to be one of the great challenges of modern life. Our society has become so complex that the average person needs to be proficient at a remarkably large number of skills. Just this week I (Bill) did a quick review of the skills I had to exercise to manage my week:

- Word processing, spreadsheet manipulation, database design, email, and web surfing
- Auto mechanics
- Landscape maintenance
- Cooking, cleaning, and laundry
- Electrical wiring repair
- Email, text messages, and voice mail from my phone
- Synchronizing my phone with my computer
- Relationship coaching over the phone
- Managing four bank accounts online
- Negotiating with a graphic designer to create a website, printed newsletter, and email broadcast.
- Organizing and running a staff meeting
- Running a training session with two employees and three volunteers

All of us exercise more skills in an average week than any previous generation did in a month or a year. With all that going on, it can be hard to figure out what skills we should master and which ones we should be content to be average at. The temptation is for everyone to be a generalist who tries to be good at everything rather than an expert who performs at the highest level in their chosen pursuit. Trying to be good at everything, however, is a black hole that can never be filled. You spend a little time here and a little time there and get frustrated with all of it. Rather than rejoice over the great accomplishments of your life, you settle into underachieving at everything.

This is the tendency the Bible is trying to fight by calling us to be athletes. Each of us has a God-given purpose. Each of us has been gifted to live out that purpose. But each of us is limited in our perspective and abilities. We aren't supposed to do everything.

Which is good, because maybe you've had a boss early in your vocational life, when you were still trying to figure out what you were best at, write a performance review like this:

- This employee works well when under constant supervision and cornered like a rat in a trap.
- This young lady has delusions of adequacy.
- He sets low personal standards and then consistently fails to achieve them.
- This employee should go far and the sooner he starts, the better.
- Got into the gene pool when the lifeguard wasn't watching.
- Bright as Alaska in December.
- If brains were taxed, she'd get a refund.
- If you give him a penny for his thoughts, you'll get change.
- It's hard to believe he beat out 1,000,000 other sperm.
- Since my last report, this employee has reached rock bottom and has started to dig.[1]

We are supposed to do something very well—and you do, so focus on it! When you focus on the achievement you were designed to accomplish, you gain energy, motivation, and dedication to do what is necessary to reach your goal.

Persistently Practice

We already mentioned that in Hebrews 12:1-3, we are called to walk in victory by focusing our sights on Jesus, who created our faith and has run the race before us. In verses 4-6, we get a stark reminder that most of life is practice: "You have not yet resisted to the point of shedding your blood... the Lord disciplines those he loves." Everyone who has ever accomplished anything worthwhile has spent enormous amounts of time and energy in preparation.

All three of our sons played four years of high school ball. We could summarize their athletic pursuits and accomplishments in a few pages, but it would not tell the real story. The real story is the hundreds of days, year after year, spent in the weight room getting stronger, countless hours doing drills to sharpen their abilities, thousands of miles on the track building endurance, and a ridiculous number of hours watching film and studying playbooks to prepare their minds for action.

We have a friend who was an alternate on the Olympic team. Just to make the *alternate* position, she had someone drive her to practice 90 minutes each way twice a day and she did her homework in the car. She practiced for over 6 hours a day every day for over 10 years. She won numerous championships along the way, but her joy in life happened each day as she hit the gym. It was her second home.

Every champion has embraced the need to spend more time at practice than he will ever spend at the game. He knows that any moments of outstanding achievement he experiences are the result of drill after drill, workout after workout, film session after film session. So the journey is just as precious to him as the win. The victory comes in the daily discipline.

This is where we discover how competitive we really are. We have been entrusted with the skills, talents, and gifts to fulfill God's purpose in our lives. Bringing the plan to fruition requires faithfulness on our part: "Now it is required that those who have been given a trust must prove faithful" (1 Corinthians 4:2). When Paul described the process of faithfulness, he said, "I discipline my body and make it my slave" (1 Corinthians 9:27).

Our bodies tend toward deterioration and can be kept in shape only through strenuous activity. Our minds tend toward selfish thinking and can be kept focused on truth only through diligent study. Our souls tend toward pride and laziness and can be kept motivated only through consistent reminders of God's grace. Our desires tend toward indulgence and self-destruction and can be kept under control only through accountability to the Holy Spirit and to fellow believers.

So in the midst of an ordinary life, what does practice look like? In order to talk about practice, we have to start with the assumption that you have some idea of what your purpose is. If that seems fuzzy for you, go back to chapter 8 and work through the steps there. Once you have identified the pursuit you are willing to invest your heart in, practice begins. It consists of training your body, mind, and will to do what is necessary.

Develop a Training Plan

If you want a long-term adventure of pursing whatever purpose God has for you, you'll want to develop a plan to maintain good health and fitness. That includes diet, exercise, sleep, and health check-ups that will enhance your effectiveness regardless of what God has called you to do.

Next, you'll want to train your mind to understand your area of interest to the highest level possible. Successful athletes spend enormous amounts of time studying game film, reviewing playbooks, and examining their technique. They live with the conviction that there's always room for improvement. This is the way you become an expert at something. If you spend a little more time and give a little more effort than other people in your area of interest, you become the go-to person in your circle of influence. Best-selling author Florence Littauer says, "Do what you do better than everyone else and you will always be a success."

These first two areas of training take effort, but they are not the hardest to work on. The toughest to train is your will. Every time you decide to grow or exercise your giftedness, your responsibility level gets bigger. More people want what you have to offer. More situations seek for your assistance. Leaders develop confidence in you and ask you to get more involved. As a result, the choice to get involved gets harder over time. At first it seems simple because the tasks are straightforward and relatively easy. Every success leads to greater opportunities, so the assignments get more complex and taxing. With each new opportunity, the will to say yes becomes a bigger challenge. If you train yourself to resist the distractions and commit to the opportunities that are vital to your interest, your will gets in line with your goals.

I (Pam) have had discussions with many successful people, such as Sheri, a producer for many of the big-name TV shows. Sheri spent several years single and successful—and lonely. She paid her dues early because she knew that someday she would want to switch her focus to things like marriage and children. She strategically worked her plan so that she moved to the top of the food chain and could decide which jobs to take, where she wanted to live, which church to attend that would help her grow most, and which projects to take that most reflected her values. It was hard on her. It required years of long hours. But she's glad she sacrificed early to gain the freedom she now enjoys.

Another of our friends stepped off the fast track in the corporate world because he believed he was giving his best hours to the office and had little time left for a social life, for serving Jesus, for travel, or even for sleep. He was afraid that if he stayed, he'd discover he was fifty, rich, and very alone. He planned his exit so he could have time to decide where he wanted to relocate and what he wanted to do for a career once he was calling his own shots.

The more specific your goals are for your *entire* life, not just your career, the more you will be able to plan out the steps to your well-rounded life.

Prepare to Reap a Harvest

The third picture in the Bible of a follower of Jesus is that of a farmer. Farmers work hard, before sunrise to after sundown. Farmers often work alone and sometimes have to get themselves out of tough situations. The farmer competes differently than the soldier and the athlete because he isn't competing against other people. The farmer competes against nature in order to raise crops. The process the farmer must follow to experience success is: (1) he must sow what he wants to reap, (2) he must pull weeds, and (3) he must provide nourishment in the form of water and fertilizer. If any of these three are missing, nature will defeat the farmer and destroy his efforts.

Success in our lives follows the same path. We must sow what we want to reap. If we want people to be compassionate, we must sow compassion into the lives of those around us. If we want influence, we must get involved with people, listen to their concerns, and seek strategies that work in real life. If we want to become a good teacher, we must learn both information and techniques to make us a proficient communicator. Whatever we want out of life, we have to invest the seeds that produce the desired results.

Then we have to fight against the obstacles that rise up to stop our progress. These obstacles come from within and without. Our old nature will look for ways to sabotage our dreams through delay, indulgence, laziness, and a hundred other self-destructive techniques. In addition, changes in procedures, unexpected demands, and financial surprises throw obstacles in the path of our pursuits. They arise as easily as weeds grow in our yards, and they are sure to arise year after year. We can either be frustrated by the weeds or we can patiently work to remove them.

Finally, every worthwhile pursuit requires nourishment. The dreams we have on our hearts require time and money to move forward. The key is to add the right amount of each at the right time to encourage growth and development. A farmer cannot add all the water and all the fertilizer on one day and expect his crops to grow. He must space out the irrigation so the plants get the right amount over time. Similarly, our goals need a ration of time and money over time in order to reach maturity and provide the harvest we dream of.

Sow to Reap

As a reminder, write down in a few words what you believe your God-given purpose is from the worksheet in chapter 8, pages 186-88:

Now, write down two things that you can do that will help you be better prepared for your pursuit (education, books, seminars, other).

1.

2.

What obstacles are you aware of and what can you do to remove them?

In the next three months, what time and money do you need to invest in your main pursuit to help it mature?

As a result of reading this book, what are the top three things God has asked you to do or top decisions He is asking you to make?

Just for Fun

If you train to be a competitor, life will seem easier.

A soldier had just returned from Afghanistan. His plans included becoming a golf course superintendent once he was discharged in a few months. He applied for a job as a greenskeeper, but the manager of the club worried that he might not be up for the job.

"It's stressful," the manager said. "You have to fight the weather, insects, and demanding club members."

"Will anyone be shooting at me while I mow the grass?" the soldier asked.

"Of course not."

"I'll take the job."

Notes

Chapter 1: Decide to Be Decisive

1. http://members.tripod.com/mi_ruka0/id9.html.
2. www.motivatingquotes.com/zig.htm.
3. http://noolmusic.com/funny_jokes/life_jokes_-_doctor.php.

Chapter 2: Decide to Walk with Jesus

1. Jim Burns HomeWord daily devotional 7/19/2010.
2. http://noolmusic.com/funny_jokes/religion_jokes_-_god_vs_the_scientists.php.

Chapter 3: Decide to Celebrate

1. www.quotegarden.com/adversity.html.
2. Ibid.
3. Ibid.
4. Ibid.
5. Ibid.
6. Ibid.
7. www.heartquotes.net/Difficulties.html.
8. www.embracehisgrace.com/Eulogeo.htm.
9. Ibid.
10. Gary L. McIntosh and Samuel D. Rima, Sr., *Overcoming the Dark Side of Leadership* (Grand Rapids, MI: Baker Books, 1997).
11. Ibid., 11.
12. Ibid., 14.
13. www.jimmyv.org/about-us/our-story.html.
14. http://en.wikipedia.org/wiki/Jim_Valvano.
15. www.anecdotage.com/index.php?aid=19043.

Chapter 4: Decide to Live in Peace

1. *Resources for further study of Temperaments:*
   Jim Brawner, *Taming the Family Zoo,* NavPress, 1998.
   The DISC Profile, www.discprofile.com or www.onlinedisc.com.
   Florence Littauer, *Personality Plus,* Fleming H. Revell Company, 1992.
   Bob Phillips, *The Delicate Art of Dancing with Porcupines*, Gospel Light Publications, 1989.
   John Trent, Rodney Cox, and Eric Tooker, *Leading from Your Strengths,* Broadman and Holman Publishers, 2004.
   Marita Littauer with Florence Littauer, *Wired That Way*, Regal Books, 2006.

2. Dave and Claudia Arp, *10 Great Dates* (Grand Rapids, MI: Zondervan, 1997), 40-41.

3. *Resources for further study on Conflict Resolution:*

    John Gottman and Nan Silver, *Seven Principles for Making Marriage Work*, Crown Publishing Group, 2000.

    John Gottman, *Why Marriages Succeed or Fail*, Simon and Schuster, 1995.

    Bill and Pam Farrel, *The Marriage Code*, Harvest House Publishers, 2010.

    Henry Cloud and John Townsend, *How to Have That Difficult Conversation You've Been Avoiding: With Your Spouse, Adult Child, Family, Boss, Coworker, Friend, Parent, or Someone You're Dating*, Zondervan, 2005.

4. *Resource for further study on Learning Styles:*

    Cynthia Tobias, *The Way They Learn*, Tyndale House Publishers, 1996.

5. *Resources for further study on Love Languages:*

    Gary Chapman, *The Five Love Languages*, Moody Publishers, 1996.

    Gary Chapman and Ross Campbell, *The Five Love Languages of Children*, Moody Publishers, 1997.

6. Kevin Leman, *The New Birth Order Book* (Grand Rapids, MI: Fleming H. Revell Company, 1998), 16.

7. *Resource for further study on Birth Order:*

    Kevin Leman, *The New Birth Order Book*, Fleming H. Revell Company, 1998.

8. *Resource for further study on Relax and Recharge Styles:*

    Bill and Pam Farrel, *Men Are Like Waffles, Women Are Like Spaghetti*, Harvest House Publishers, 2001.

9. *Resources for further study on Gifts:*

    Larry Gilbert, *Spiritual Gifts Inventory*, http://store.churchgrowth.org/epages/ChurchGrowth.sf.

    Elmer Towns, "Spiritual Gift Questionnaire," http://elmertowns.com/spiritual_gifts_test/.

    C. Peter Wagner, *Discover Your Spiritual Gifts*, Regal Books, 2005.

    "Spiritual Gifts Survey," Lifeway Christian Resources, 2003, www.lifeway.com/lwc/files/lwcF_wmn_SpiritualGifts_Survey.pdf. This resource can help you create a chart that shows how high you score on each gift.

10. *Resources for further study on Financial Styles:*

    Ellie Kay, *A Woman's Guide to Family Finances*, Bethany House Publishers, 2003.

    Bill and Pam Farrel, *The Marriage Code*, Harvest House Publishers, 2010.

11. *Resources for further study on Parenting Styles:*

    Dave Arp and Claudia Arp, *And Suddenly They're Thirteen*, Zondervan, 1999.

    James Dobson, *The New Dare to Discipline*, Tyndale House Publishers, 1996.

    James Dobson, *The New Strong-Willed Child*, Tyndale House Publishers, 2004.

    Bill and Pam Farrel, *The 10 Best Decisions a Parent Can Make*, Harvest House Publishers, 2001.

12. www.inspireme.net/funny_stories/salary_increase.htm.

Chapter 5: Decide to Wait

1. www.guy-sports.com/humor/stories/story_supermarket_teacher.htm.

Chapter 6: Decide to Define Relationships

1. Leslie Vernick, *The Emotionally Destructive Relationship* (Eugene, OR: Harvest House Publishers, 2007), 27-28.

2. Joe S. McIlhaney Jr., MD, and Freda McKissic Bush, MD, *Hooked: New Science on How Casual Sex Is Affecting Our Children* (Chicago: Northfield Publishing: 2008), 16.

3. Marian Wallace and Vanessa Warner, "Abstinence: Why Sex Is Worth the Wait," Concerned Women for America, 5 September 2002, www.cwfa.org/printerfriendly.asp?id=1195&department=cwa&categoryid=family.

4. McIlhaney and Bush, *Hooked*, 31-33.

5. Ibid., 35.

6. Ibid., 43.

7. Dave Carder, *Close Calls* (Chicago: Northfield Publishing, 2008), quoted in ibid., 69.

8. Ibid., 81.

9. Ibid., 117.

10. Wallace and Warner, "Abstinence."

11. Bill and Pam Farrel, *Red-Hot Monogamy* (Eugene, OR: Harvest House Publishers, 2006).

12. Barbara Wilson, *Kiss Me Again: Restoring Lost Intimacy in Marriage* (Colorado Springs: Multnomah Books, 2009), 45.

13. Bill and Pam Farrel, *Single Men Are like Waffles, Single Women Are like Spaghetti* (Eugene, OR: Harvest House Publishers, 2002).

14. McIlhaney and Bush, *Hooked*, 98.

15. Wallace and Warner, "Abstinence."

16. Lambert Dolphin, "Masturbation and the Bible," www.ldolphin.org/Mast.shtml.

17. www.answerbag.com/q_view/623955.

18. http://funsms.net/friendship_jokes.htm.

Chapter 7: Decide to Live the Good Life

1. Chris Houston, "How Many Millionaires Are There in the United States?" Associated Content, 20 July 2009, www.associatedcontent.com/article/1962738/how_many_millionaires_are_there_in.html.

2. www.americandebtadvisor.com/questions/howmanyamericansareindebt.shtml.

3. "Americans' Reliance on Credit Leads Many into Debt," *PBS NewsHour*, 18 August 2008, www.pbs.org/newshour/bb/business/july-dec08/personaldebt_08-18.html.

4. Bob Lawless, "Projected Bankruptcy Filings in 2009," Credit Slips, 18 December 2008, www.creditslips.org/creditslips/2008/12/bankruptcy-filings-in-2009.html.

5. Georgia Shaffer, *Taking Out Your Emotional Trash* (Eugene, OR: Harvest House Publishers, 2010), 13-14.

6. *Fox News*, 17 July 2010.

7. www.firstplace4health.com/stories/48/becky_turner.

8. Arlene Pellicane, *31 Days to a Younger You* (Eugene, OR: Harvest House Publishers, 2011), 118.

9. Pam Farrel, *The 10 Best Decisions a Woman Can Make* (Eugene OR: Harvest House Publishers, 1999), 169.

10. See Carole Lewis, *Give God a Year, Change Your Life Forever!* (Ventura, CA: Regal Books, 2009).

11. Personal email from Christin Ditchfield to Pam Farrel.

12. Becky Turner personal email to Pam Farrel, June 2010.

Chapter 8: Decide to Be an Influencer

1. Adapted from Pam Farrel, *Woman of Influence* (Eugene, OR: Harvest House Publishers, 2009).

Chapter 9: Decide to Be a Communicator

1. www.gomilpitas.com/humor/122.htm.

2. For more information on nonverbal communication, see www.helpguide.org/mental/EQ6_nonverbal_communication.htm.

Chapter 10: Decide to Be a Competitor

1. www.bullyonline.org/successunlimited/humour/jokes.htm.

For more resources to enhance your relationships
and build marriages or to connect with Bill and Pam Farrel
for a speaking engagement, contact

Farrel Communications
Masterful Living Ministries
3755 Avocado Boulevard, #414
La Mesa, CA 91941

800-810-4449

info@farrelcommunications.com

www.farrelcommunications.com

For help with marriage issues in midlife, visit
www.seasonedsisters.com

Other Great Harvest House Books
by Bill and Pam Farrel

MEN ARE LIKE WAFFLES—
WOMEN ARE LIKE SPAGHETTI
Bill and Pam Farrel

Bill and Pam explain why a man is like a waffle (each element of his life is in a separate box), why a woman is like spaghetti (everything in her life touches everything else), and what these differences mean. Then they show readers how to achieve more satisfying relationships. Biblical insights, sound research, humorous anecdotes, and real-life stories make this guide entertaining and practical. Readers will feast on enticing insights that include

- letting gender differences work for them
- achieving fulfillment in romantic relationships
- coordinating parenting so kids receive good, consistent care

Much of the material in this rewarding book will also improve interactions with family, friends, and coworkers.

MEN ARE LIKE WAFFLES—
WOMEN ARE LIKE SPAGHETTI STUDY GUIDE
Bill and Pam Farrel

This easy-to-use study guide will take you to a new level in your appreciation of the differences and special delights of your mate. Designed to address the important issues of a happy marriage, this guide will

- make planning time with each other fun and exciting
- help you and your mate coordinate parenting so your kids get the best
- bring out the best you have to give in sex, romance, and communication

This guide is great for leading couples in biblically based discussions or for couples to use on their own to create their own marriage retreat.

SINGLE MEN ARE LIKE WAFFLES—
SINGLE WOMEN ARE LIKE SPAGHETTI
Bill and Pam Farrel

Do you wonder how to relate to the opposite sex? Do you want to build a stronger relationship with your girlfriend or boyfriend? In this great book, Bill and Pam help "waffles" and "spaghettis" explore

- how to meet other singles
- the advantages and disadvantages of being male and female
- what to do if you're single again with kids

Discover how a relationship with God can fulfill your key needs. A discussion guide is included for small group or personal use.

RED-HOT MONOGAMY:
MAKING YOUR MARRIAGE SIZZLE
Bill and Pam Farrel

Did you know that the best sexual experiences are enjoyed by married couples? Bill and Pam reveal how you can add spark and sizzle to your love life. You'll discover how

- God specifically designed you to give and receive pleasure from your mate
- a little skill turns marriage into red-hot monogamy
- sex works best emotionally, physically, and physiologically

Along with ways to create intimacy when you're just too tired and how to avoid the "pleasure thieves," this book offers hundreds more ideas to inspire romance and passion in every aspect of your lives together.

The 10 Best Decisions a Couple Can Make

Bill and Pam Farrel

Use this tool chest of communication skills to get the most out of your marriage. You'll quickly connect with the home-improvement theme as you discover how to

- strengthen the foundation of your family
- inspect your marriage for hidden weak spots
- protect your relationship with consistent care and improvement

Filled with practical advice, biblical insights, warmth, and wit, this manual is perfect for newlyweds as well as longtime marriage partners.

The 10 Best Decisions Every Parent Can Make

Bill and Pam Farrel

The parents of three active children, Bill and Pam know what they're talking about in this book filled with personal experience, wisdom, and encouragement. The Farrels offer specific ideas for loving and nurturing your children, including prodigals and those with special needs or strong wills.

Packed with creative, motivational tools and games that allow children to blossom and succeed, this book will help your children become everything God designed them to be.

The 10 Best Decisions a Woman Can Make
Pam Farrel

Pam encourages you to exchange the fleeting standards of the world for the steadfast truths found in a growing, fruitful relationship with God. You'll discover the joy of finding your place in God's plan as you

- realize how precious you are to the Lord
- find a positive place to direct your creativity, energy, and enthusiasm
- gain confidence regarding the value of your time and efforts

Pam's warm, motivating message will touch your heart as you seek all God has for you.

The 10 Best Decisions a Man Can Make
Bill Farrel

You have important decisions to make that affect your family, your career, and your ministry. Sometimes the choices seem overwhelming, and you end up taking the path of least resistance. Let Bill Farrel give you the hands-on decision-making tools you need to make the kinds of choices you won't regret. You'll experience the satisfaction of finding your place in God's plan as you

- make better decisions with less stress
- improve your relationships
- increase your influence in the areas that matter most

The 10 Best Decisions a Man Can Make will empower you to pursue God's best and to achieve true success in the adventure of your life.

WOMAN OF CONFIDENCE
Pam Farrel

Pam helps you discover that nothing is more vital to your self-confidence than your confidence in God. Your ability to achieve, to move through life with courage and boldness, rests on the character, power, and strength of God. Develop the confidence you need to walk into your hopes, dreams, and aspirations.

Great for your women's group or for personal encouragement.

FANTASTIC AFTER FORTY!
The Savvy Woman's Guide to Her Best Season of Life
Pam Farrel

Pam offers words of encouragement, challenge, and humor for women between the ages of 40 and 60. Her 40 ways to forge a fulfilling future include

- take control of health and maximize energy
- embrace God's power and truth and experience renewal
- discover your uniqueness to live your purpose

Designed for personal or group study, this empowering read is just the beginning of Pam's conversation with baby-boomer women who desire life-enhancing resources and who want to pass them along to other women.

To learn more about other Harvest House books
or to read sample chapters, log on to our website:

www.harvesthousepublishers.com

HARVEST HOUSE PUBLISHERS
EUGENE, OREGON